Be blessed
as you
read
this!

Thank God,
My Parents Died

By

Judith van Tonder

INFINITY
PUBLISHING.COM

Copyright © 2009 by Judith van Tonder

ISBN 0-7414-5287-1

Published by:

INFI∞ITY
PUBLISHING.COM

1094 New DeHaven Street, Suite 100
West Conshohocken, PA 19428-2713
Info@buybooksontheweb.com
www.buybooksontheweb.com
Toll-free (877) BUY BOOK
Local Phone (610) 941-9999
Fax (610) 941-9959

Printed in the United States of America

Published May 2010

Acknowledgments

Book cover and design Michael van Tonder
Author Photographer Michael van Tonder
Editor Vicky Bell

This Memoir Is Dedicated To:

You, my God, for giving me the courage to write this. I crawled in pain and agony as the memories ate at my soul. You picked me up. You helped me to GIVE what I never RECEIVED, love in abundance.

Keith, thank you for all the loving years being married to you. We met when I was in the Children's Home and you loved me regardless. You persuaded me to write it all down.

My Michelle, first born and precious baby-girl, Jesus placed you in my arms and heart, you are my angel, who is all grown-up now and still gives me joy, love and support.

My Michael, our son born three years later and added laughter to the love triangle, you made our family complete. Your encouragement, support and artistic addition to the memoir helped me look good, Thanks my boetie!

Thank you my three, you are my life!

I would also like to thank the people who played a 'roll' in my upbringing, mostly the black women from South Africa, they have this amazing instinctive love for children and I copied how they did it, with my own, thank you.

Contents

Prologue

I trailed my hand along the seams of the brown suitcase. It was worn and old, but I could count the neat stitches if I wanted, which would help the time go by.

I placed both my palms on the suitcase and looked at the sweaty prints they left on the brown cardboard. My head was so empty, so strangely quiet.

Inside this brown suitcase was just what the children's home had given me: Two skirts, one blouse, one jersey, a bra, three panties and a pair of pyjamas. Oh, yes, and two Bibles. One I had received at my confirmation in the Dutch Reformed Church. The other was the little blue one, in English, with my name written on the front page: Judy Alexander. I hid this little Bible; it was my secret reminder of the life I had endured when I was kidnapped.

All these years in the children's home and this was what I had to show for it? Well, I had come into this place empty handed, so why should I have accumulated anything? It was just borrowed; they had made that clear enough to us.

I was sitting on the edge of the bed and began thinking of how all this had happened to me. How my life's walk had progressed to where I was now, leaving the children's home for the very last time. I was eighteen years old, enough to start life on my own. I would leave these burglar bars behind, and just the thought of that made me breathe a little easier.

I looked over to the window and saw the familiar metal bars. They had kept me locked inside for too long. God knew I had hated this place for a long, long time.

CHAPTER ONE

My Life

I was born into this world in Stellenbosch, South Africa, on a sunny day in 1957. My mother winced and hated every moment of the childbirth. She told me years later, I was lucky because I was the second child; my poor brother had a bigger struggle, because the doctors had to remove him using force and biceps from my mother's womb. She just did not want to go through childbirth, and since she hated my father and she believed she was going through this as a result of his lust, she simply hated him and me for it.

I was a happy, fat and contented baby who smiled a lot. I had a head of curly blonde hair and blue eyes. I took to the breast and I was not sickly or fussy.

There were three of us, born precisely three years apart. We lived in Stellenbosch for a time, but my father got into fistfights with the University students every weekend in the bars, and the fact that this area was in the wine region did not help, so we were forced to leave. We ended up in Lesotho, on a piggery where my father convinced the farmer he knew everything about farming, and what he did not know, he was prepared to learn. During one of my parents' fighting fits, I heard my mother tell my father that all he knew about pigs was how to devour the chops she had to cook for him and take to him in bed, where he ate and drank.

The sun shone bright on one particular lazy Saturday afternoon. The shops had closed at one p.m. Silence stretched out over the dusty roads of the small village in Lesotho. A dove lingered, checking me out as I shifted my feet through the red, dusty sand.

I was sitting on the last step of the red polished veranda when I heard him coming. This was our Saturday ritual; he would be carrying that transistor radio on his shoulder, singing along with the African township music. I was excited, because this shiny black man had the most beautiful face and the whitest of teeth, and his rhythm and dancing made me smile. He, too, knew I was waiting for him and took his time to walk by. The excitement was building in my head and I waited in anticipation, but looked cautiously towards the windows, behind which I knew my father was sleeping. He had drunk beer since early today, so he would be asleep for a while.

The music was in my head and tears of joy made me laugh into the black man's face; he was in a good mood today and took an extra bow as he slipped around the corner of the street and away.

It was over; another week would have to go by for me to be this happy again. Dusting my feet off on the torn piece of towel at the front door, I crept inside the house to await another horrific night with my parents fighting and scolding; a few pieces of furniture might even fly.

Things did seem better for a while, except that my father was an artist; he did not want to get his hands dirty. He tried to pretend he could do it, but this life was strange to him. He wanted to do window dressing in the city and not live a rural farming life. The day he left for good on that donkey cart with his suit on, I knew he had had enough.

My mother moved us to Kroonstad and started a life without her abusive husband, trying to support her three children. Petrus was a baby, I was about four years old, and Francois was three years older than me.

This is the story of my life.

CHAPTER TWO

How It Started

I was five years old, holding onto the legs of the dining table, kicking and screaming as the welfare worker tried to take us away from my mother. My mother drank too much when she was not at work. She held three jobs to feed us, the thin white kids, aged two, five and eight.

This welfare woman was trying to pull me out from under the table, calling and coaxing me to cooperate, and then I sunk my teeth into her pale, white-stocking leg. With a yell and a jump, she went flying out of the door to get some help.

"These bloody kids have turned into animals! We should get the animal cruelty society for them, rather than putting them in a place of care!"

I turned and peeped out from under the table to look into her eyes, and all I saw was hatred and repulsion. But I didn't care; all I wanted was to stay with my mother and my two brothers.

The welfare lady and her assistant drove off in her white Volkswagen Beetle.

My older brother came crawling out of the broom cupboard, grinning.

"Well hidden, my boy," my mother said to him as she swayed my younger brother from one hip to the other.

We had gone through this many times, and it was easy and fun to place the fear into those welfare people's hearts. I knew my mother was proud of us; she told us they were the enemy, teaching us to feel superior to these people.

"What will happen to those kids, only God knows!" They would shake their heads and ponder all the scenarios we would end up in when we grew up.

My mother was too scared now to ask for financial help, because every time, it led to an attempt to take us away, so she held down three jobs. One was to pay the black maid who took care of us when my mother was at work, and the other two were to make ends meet. Her uniform for the evening job amazed me: it was all black and white with a little bowtie; she ushered people to their seats at the cinema. She worked like this for two years after leaving Lesotho, with no contact or support from my father.

It was her day job at the O.K. Bazaars that took me away from them.

All three kids were in bed with the measles on a warm, rainy November day in Kroonstad. We were to stay in bed and were red and itchy, and I know I complained a lot. I was upset when my mother took washing pegs and hung blankets in front of all the windows. I got anxious when I couldn't see outside, I told her, but she remained steadfast: "You'll go blind if you look into the sunlight when you have the measles," she said. This reassured me for a while, because I was frightened about losing any of my senses. I had seen a blind man and decided that was the worst thing I have seen.

But the itching continued and Sara, our maid, complained to my mother about my behaviour. "This little girl, aikona, this is the difficult one—she does not lie still and she is the big trouble all the time. The boys, they are the good boys," she would say, and click her tongue in frustration.

This made my mother so angry with me and she made me promise to be a good girl; then she would add, "Don't be like your bloody father!" Then followed all the saddest words as she described how hard it was for her to keep food on our plates and how she hated my lazy father and how I was spoilt and bad.

That same afternoon, a lady came home with my mother. Mrs. Isabel Alexander was there because of me. I knew it the moment she set her brown eyes on me. I shrunk under the blankets, watching and listening to every word, my hands curled into balls, and I became aware later of the same feeling of apprehension when people look at me this way, frowning.

Mrs. Alexander was the head of personnel at the O.K. Bazaar stores for which my mother worked. Mrs. Alexander said she would love to give me a summer vacation over the December holidays. She would bring me back in time and help buy my new school clothes for the start of the school year, which begins in January in South Africa. I turned six years old and was old enough to start school at the beginning of the following year.

I lived for the moment of going to school like my big brother, Francois, because he had all the answers, and I knew he had learnt them at school. I was itchy and hot in the bed and could not care about the plans. My mother did not look too excited, so it didn't seem to be too big a deal.

After getting better, we were allowed outside again. I resumed my daily rituals of play when Francois went off to school in the morning, and while the nanny took care of my younger brother, I would be left to the wonder world I had discovered.

It consisted of the passages between the flats, the alleys where no one but I would while the morning away. I found treasures discarded out of the rows of bathroom windows that rose above my head. People threw amazing stuff away; I even found a shilling, on one occasion. The maid said I should give it to her for milk or else we would drink black coffee. She was right; I remembered one morning when my mother never came home the night before and the maid woke us by knocking at the door, just to tell us this was a black coffee morning. She clicked her tongue many times that morning and I knew she was upset, but she stood looking at us with sad eyes and poured extra sugar into our black coffees. My illegitimate brother was conceived that night, the one I never knew. He was the one who was never spoken of, as if it had never happened.

I discovered razor blades that people had thrown out of their bathroom windows. They were beautiful when you stacked them up into neat little piles. I would shine them up first with the hem of my dress, and then I would walk out of the shadowed alley to show them off to the sun.

They were fine and sparkled in the light and it made me smile. I would sit cross-legged and trace little incisions into the tips of my fingers; I realised I was fearless and had no pain as droplets of red blood filtered out of my white skin, perfect little rows of cuts, perfectly spaced. I would think of the story my brother had told about the red drops of blood in the snow; I had never seen snow, but the drops of blood on the white pavement were the same, and I felt as beautiful as the girl in the story.

CHAPTER THREE
Mrs. Alexander

As I drove off with Mrs. Alexander in her beige Mercedes in early December, a feeling of resignation came over me. My mother had told me many times not to go off with strangers or, worse, with my father, if he came by; now she was allowing exactly that to happen to me. I was driving off with a stranger.

I looked back and saw the little blonde heads next to each other. They were standing in front of the apartment building, behind the gate; the gate was closed as if that was the cause of our separation. My older brother had an angry look on his face. He was so clever, and if he did not like the idea of me going off, I knew it was a bad idea.

I had asked him one day, when he came home from school, if God was a man or a woman.

He went to sit on his haunches and frowned. "Well, that, Judy, we will never know."

He looked so serious, so I bumped him off his haunches because I knew he actually wanted to pee, and I ran off as he chased me. "I love him so much because he is so clever!" I thought.

Now I looked back once more, but could not see them anymore.

Mrs. Alexander asked me if I liked dogs. I said yes, because I knew what to answer when a trick question came along. I knew she had dogs because of all the hair on the blanket on the back seat.

I sulked and she tried to reassure me that my life would be better now. On her dashboard was a silver medallion of a man walking with a shepherd's cane and a baby on his shoulders. Mrs. Alexander told me the story of Saint Christopher. I loved her soft, musical voice. She had a golden piece in her front tooth, gold bracelets, gold buttons on her navy jacket and swinging gold earrings, and I knew she was rich.

I must have fallen asleep while she told me the story, because I woke as she drove into a neat driveway under a pergola hung extravagantly with grapes. The most beautiful little house was visible as we climbed out the car; it had a rose garden and the grass was very green and perfect. There was a huge patterned mat at the front door. I wiped my feet like Mrs. Alexander did as we entered.

"Welcome home," she said, and led me into the house.

The first face I saw I fell in love with.

"Rosa, this is Nonnatjie [Miss] Judy." She introduced me to the little black maid, who had a wide, toothless smile. "Sy's Afrikaans soos jy, Rosa" ("She's Afrikaans like you, Rosa").

"Hello," I said, feeling uncomfortable. She took my plastic shopping bag of clothes to my room, and I fell in love with a green palace. I normally hated green, but this was what you would see on those Russel's Furniture pamphlets I always stared at, when they lay all over the floor in front of the mailboxes in the entrance to the flats.

Then the bulldogs came to greet me. They were slobbering and tail- wagging and made the most awful sounds, but I saw their smiles and smiled back, trying not to get any of the spit on me.

"Oh, you'll get used to their saliva, and it won't bother you as much," Mrs. Alexander said, kissing her dogs affection-ately and speaking in a language I had never heard; I decided it must be dog-love language.

"Now it's time for tea," she said, and I saw for the first time that Mrs. Alexander did not walk, she floated, gently and light-footed off into the lounge. I, of course, came plonking along with my long, thin legs and sat down. It was all so dreamlike, a dream from which I could not awake.

The tea was not sweet and white like my mother's, and there were no Marie biscuits or rusks to dunk. Instead we had soft brown bread sandwiches, which were good. I was so very, very hungry and ate quite a few.

"Wow, you can eat a lot," was all she said, and I was sure I saw a disapproving look.

I would see that look a lot in my future.

I thought it was just Mrs. Alexander, Rosa and I, but then she told me she had an older son who was in boarding school. And then there was another person, Rose. Aunty Rose, she introduced herself. She had short black hair, all slicked back like a man. She was also dressed so differently from Mrs. A. She wore a slack suit and flat, manlike shoes. It was her heart I loved: she was real and kind and told me to ask her anything I needed to know, and if I was uncertain, she was there for me.

It was Aunty Rose who took me for a bath that evening. I said I could manage fine, but she insisted, since she had bought me new pyjamas and wanted to help me with that. I could not remember any time in my life when someone had bathed me, but this felt good.

She ran the bathwater so deep I thought I might drown. She sprinkled rose-coloured crystals into the water; the smell was so new and sweet and it suited Aunty Rose's name. The steam of the bath swirled throughout the space and I could see myself walking in a haze of pink roses. The cleanest smell tickled my nose and I felt like floating away.

As I stood there in this trance, she asked me if anyone had touched me in a strange, uncomfortable way.

"I always bathe myself," I replied.

"No, I mean has your daddy touched you in a bad way, over there?" She pointed to my privates, asking this so matter-of-factly I could not understand. "You see, some daddies do this, and I want to know if your daddy has done that to you."

"I don't know." I realised it was a trick question and I knew how to answer those.

"Well, Judy, if you remember, then you should tell me." With this, she lathered up the face cloth with so many soapy bubbles and started washing me, with instructions. "First we start from the top and work our way down, because it is from clean to dirty that we wash."

I was amazed how she showed me the space that lay behind my ears, and I discovered my elbows and little knobs on my wrists I had never seen before. We played the train game. The lathered, soapy cloth became the train and travelled around my body which, in turn, became the world. When she approached my privates, she refreshed the soapy cloth and put it in my hand with instructions; she said the only person to wash the secret caves was the owner, and I did it.

She made me laugh, going over my ticklish knees, and then the rinsing and drying became another game of fun and stories, which made me cry out in laughter. As she placed me like a parcel into, first, the soft and fluffy towel, and then the soft flannel pyjamas with the little printed trains, my head was spinning and I felt like I never had in my life before.

She hugged me when we were finished and said she loved me already.

That night I dreamt of trains going through the softest mountains and woke only once, when the trains approached the cave. I wiped my eyes and looked over at the door, but there was nobody and I was still in my green room. I wiped my hands over the flannel trains on my pyjamas and sighed contentedly.

CHAPTER FOUR
How I Was Stolen

My mother insisted on seeing me on Christmas Day and Mrs. A. obliged. I could feel this was not a good trip. My tummy was in knots and I felt strange in my new clothes. What would my mother say?

I had on a pleated Scottish tartan skirt and I knew my brother was going to laugh at the big nappy pin on the front of it. My hair was slicked out of all its curls and pulled into a tight, high ponytail. The ribbon, dangling from the bits of blonde, was the exact plaid of my skirt. I knew my mother loved bright pinks, and that now I looked like "those" people. I hoped she would still love me, but looking like I was, I knew she might not approve of me at all.

The afternoon turned into a disaster as the two women glared and snarled at each other. My mother cut slices of the pink and lime green cake with a proud smile. Francois pulled my hair and I was out of the bobby socks and shoes as soon as he laughed.

My little brother vomited bits of cake over Mrs. A's navy shoes and my mother rushed with a dirty brown rag to wipe it up. In an instant I felt embarrassed for the sake of my mother and knew Mrs. A was looking down on her. I could see why and hated myself for those thoughts.

The glares continued and my mother decided I should not continue my visit with Mrs. A, but come home to live with her and the boys again; Mrs. A could mail my belongings back to her.

"How can you take care of all three now?" Mrs. A enquired as she lifted one eyebrow into an arch.

"You see, my husband returned and he has a good window-dressing job—we are going to be fine!" I heard the pitch in Mother's voice and understood the blue mark under her jaw.

The two women were now into a full-blown argument. I could see the hatred in my mother's eyes. In return, wet droplets appeared on Mrs. A's top lip as her face turned cold.

I was still eyeing the unopened gifts wrapped in the shiniest of paper under the little plastic tree when I was scooped up by Mrs. A. She stuffed me into the car and threw the shoes and socks onto my lap. The whole time, I felt my mother's claw digging into my wrist through the open window. I heard her scream death threats towards Mrs. A.

Foam was dripping onto my white blouse. I saw it was coming from my mother's mouth. For the first time in my life, I felt frozen in my bones; I had no idea what to do. Was I to get out of the car and run towards my screaming brother urging me to get out the car to come to them? Should I stay in the car and pull my mother's fingers off me, or should I jump out now and I run to hide behind my brother? My little brother was turning blue from crying and not catching his breath in time, and I knew my mother needed to get to him.

I pleaded for my mother to look at him. "Mamma, Petrus word blou!" ("Mummy, Petrus is turning blue!").

My mother was speaking into my face and I smelt the drops of spit, heavy with wine, as they exploded on my skin. "You get out of this car or I will kill you today!"

I don't exactly remember how, but I felt the car pull into motion. I don't know if it was true or not, but my mother shouted that Mrs. A had driven over her foot. At this stage we had a crowd of neighbours staring at the Christmas spectacle.

I shrunk into a pathetic ball on the seat and did not look back at my brother, afraid of what I might see in his eyes.

I left them. Whenever Petrus turned blue, it was I who would always help him come right and regain his breath. Had I killed him? Had I made Mother cry and drink until the welfare came for both my brothers and took them away? Every day I thought of them and what I had done. I had deserted them and my dad must have been so angry when he did not find me home that he would have killed my mother. Now I would be without a mother. Maybe Mrs. A would become my mother and I would ask her to give my brothers a home here with me, too.

I knew to pray for them, and at night, when I was snug in my train pyjamas, I would slip out of bed onto my knees and pray with all my might that God would help my brothers.

I started school in a new language, English. I was going to a convent school. It was a privilege. I was to greet the nuns by calling them Sister. I did not know where I was the first day, and to make matters worse, I did not understand what these people were saying.

I thought I would never make friends and tell stories because they did not speak Afrikaans. Before they prayed, they would touch their heads and hearts with their hands, making the cross, so I did it too. I copied everything. I studied everything and watched their every move. I would mimic these girls in front of the mirror at home and studied English with all my heart. Mrs. A sent me to elocution lessons, and I practiced non-stop the Betty-went-to-buy-a-pound-of butter, but-the-bit-of-butter-Betty-bought-was-bitter, so-Betty-bought-another-bit-of-butter, to-make-the-bitter-butter-better.

My days became a miasma of nuns and crosses and incense and the priest with his golden dresses. I followed and imitated and lost myself, trying to be a new person. I did not know myself anymore. I looked different, I wore shoes. I had tight plaits and a strange tongue.

It was in the afternoons, after school, that my life became mine. Rosa would have the most wonderful warm plate of food ready for me as I walked into the kitchen. The aroma of lamb chops would greet me at the garden gate and I would run up the steps and into the house. The woman with the toothless smile would hug me and laugh as I danced with this little black crow. She would playfully smack me on the bottom and send me to take off the school uniform. Then I would tuck into the softest green beans and whitest mashed potatoes and sit back and tell Rosa what fantastic food she had created and that I would love her until the end of the world.

She would dish up a warm dessert of peaches and custard and pour the liquid cream over it and allow me to take it outside to eat, sitting on the polished veranda.

I would escape into the garden and play with my new imaginary English friends. They loved me and I spoke fluently and ran between the trees. Rosa would help me tie strings to my short ponytail, and these long waves of hair would float with me through the garden. I was happy.

Then the evenings would come and bring Mrs. A home.

Rosa would have me straightened out upon her arrival home. I would sit neatly after my bath at the table and practise my times tables. With an arched eyebrow, Mrs. A would seat herself next to me and I was so scared.

I could feel Rosa's down-turned eyes as she busied herself at the basin with the dishes. My heart would beat so fast and hard I was sure you could see the movement under my clothes. I would have known all my spelling and times table a minute ago, but now my head seemed so hazy with fright, I forgot it all. I crossed my legs but still I would feel the trickle run down, and this would be the cause of everything that followed: the anger, the disappointment. Why would I pee in my pants when Rosa forced me go to the toilet a dozen times before Mrs. A came home? Still, it happened, and it caused the wrath, which followed.

My stinging legs afterward. Lying in the bed without supper, crying because I felt so alone. The red fingerprints swelling on my legs. I would rub them softly and tell myself not to cry, it was going to be all right. As I rubbed my legs, I would realise they didn't sting as much as that look of disapproval. I had not tried hard enough; I must just try again tomorrow.

I would hear my door open softly and I shut my eyes to make as if I were sleeping. Aunty Rose would kiss my forehead and I could feel the wet of her sadness on my skin. I heard them fight; I heard their anger and I knew it was my fault. The next day, Rosa would put an extra Marmite sandwich in my lunch box, which would make me smile again, and as I ran into the house after school, she would be there with her little black midget arms open for me to run into.

I would slip out of the bed onto the floor on my knees and forget to make the sign of the cross; I prayed for Francois and Petrus; that was, if Petrus was still alive and I had not killed him by my leaving.

One Saturday morning, Mrs. A and Rosa grabbed me and stuffed me into a wardrobe in Mrs. A's bedroom. My father had come to fetch me; I heard his voice at the front door and the shouting. I prayed for him not to find me. I could not make out what was being said, but there was a lot of screaming and I did hear the threats of the police, and it made me scared. On the lapel of the coat rubbing against my body in the cupboard was a brooch with sharp, thin edges, which cut into my fingers as I kept sliding my hands over it and cried, pee trickling down my legs.

*   *   *

I looked out the train's window; I saw the wide, open landscape of the Free State. The vast openness and changes of colour whispering from the furthest purple blue where the sky touched the horizon; the entire landscape was segmented with lines, the "koppies" (small hills) came next, and then the next horizontal line, which was grey green with deep, red-brown spots, the red of the earth peeking through. Further down, my eyes were met with a shy, soft, immense green.

I sighed and thought of this wingspan of freedom. How was it possible that in this free openness of landscape of the Free State, I had been locked up for so long, the imprisonment of a child spirit? I felt the rhythm of the steam train and the click of the metal rails. It was singing in my ears, the refrain of "I-must, I-must, I-must-get-away", and I started a game: each blade of grass I focused on and stone nearby I saw right then I would never see again. I would never have to come back this way again.

This was now behind me, and with every "click" of the railway track, I was another click further away from my sad past. I could now dust "Ons Kinderhuis" (Our Children's Home) off from my being and build my own new future.

My hatred was as vast as this landscape and my pain deeper than this red earth. I trailed my finger along the seam of my brown suitcase and allowed myself to think for a moment of a life before the children's home.

CHAPTER FIVE
The Hungry Years

I felt myself float into such a new, hazy state. We packed up in Bloemfontein. Mrs. A had a plan; I overheard her tell Rosa that it was the only way. Mrs. A. and Aunty Rose were going to take me away where nobody would find me.

I saw Rosa cock her little black head to the side, looking at the paper Mrs. A was waving in front of old Rosa's face. I knew Rosa could not read and Mrs. A must have realised her mistake, because she started to explain the most evil of letters burning in her hand.

"The interdict in my hand is from the bloody authorities that want me to give her back to her pathetic parents!" At the words "pathetic parents", I saw her red lips part in disgust.

Well, because of me, we were now on our way to Pretoria. Rosa stayed behind because she could not live that far away from her only son, also called Francois.

I looked into her brown eyes as I clung to her apron. She was crying soft, wet drops onto my face. I hugged her hard, praying I could disappear into her black skin, become one with Rosa and be her all at the same time.

This prayer did not come true, because I felt Mrs. A's strong arms tear me from her. I looked back at Rosa's little crooked arm waving at me, wiping her eyes on toilet paper. "I love you, Rosa, forever," I whispered into my sobs.

"Blow your nose, Judy. Pull yourself together." Mrs. A's arched brow shot a look at me in the rear-view mirror.

Aunty Rose passed me her soft, white handkerchief and a gentle smile. I crawled into a ball on the seat and the bulldogs licked my face. I lay back between the dogs and was introduced to my soul flies and spirit.

They were little fireflies; but more than small, shining lights, they were lights of different colours. I had never seen fireflies, but I presumed this was what they must look like. All of them flew around my head; most flew out of the window. It was the blue ones that lingered behind; they smiled at me and touched my face. These were the peaceful ones, the ones that dried up tears and granted me only one sigh of sadness. Later I would realise it was the yellow ones that stayed with me at all times; the blue bits of peace were only there when my heart was totally broken into pieces. They would pick up the pieces with swift but gentle gestures and patch it all up again. I could nearly always stop crying when they finished their job. They were my sweet and pacifying little bits of spirit, and for years I would need them more than any of the other colours.

We moved into a pretty little house with a giant palm tree in the front garden. It was close to the Prime Minister's house, but you could never see his place, as it was far, far in the back of his very big garden. Mrs. A was very proud of living so close to him; this made me proud, too.

This was the first part of my hungry years. My days at school were weird and I seemed to be in trouble most of the time. I was in an Afrikaans school and this helped: I could understand the teachers and we did not make the sign of the cross before we prayed. I had to catch myself not to do it. The teacher told us the Catholics were way off the religious track and their rituals would get them straight into hell. This frightened me right out of the old habit of making the cross. I did not tell Mrs. A the teacher had said this, because she would have sorted this teacher out with her very swift tongue.

After school, I would walk across the Apies River, over the most beautiful little bridge, to Masie, Mrs. A's mother. She lived in flats where mostly old people lived. Masie was sweet and kind and, I think, a little scared of her daughter, just like me. We had this unspoken fear in common, which created a special bond. She would look as unsettled as I felt when the time approached for Mrs. A to collect me after her day at work.

Masie gave me soup in a cup for lunch. It was mostly tomato soup from a sachet stirred with boiling water from the kettle, because she did not have a kitchen. Masie would put my crackers in a row on a little plate. I was still always hungry, and I savoured the last cracker, but I knew Masie did not have much money, so I would not ask for more to eat. We settled into a nice routine of listening to the stories on the radio and doing my homework in the afternoons. She made me practise my writing skills over and over, until I wrote big, beautiful letters just like the other girls in my class. Masie had soft, wrinkly hands, and I loved to touch them and run my fingers over her beautiful, neat, oval nails.

My days in school were hard. The children looked at me strangely and I always understood why. I called the woman I lived with "tannie" (aunty) and did not do as well as they did at schoolwork. I always got into trouble for not paying attention. I had so many dreams in my head, filling my thoughts and taking my attention away from the teacher and schoolwork.

These girls hated me, but that just made me angry and aggressive towards them and I hated them back. I was sent to the corner at the back of the class for chatting to the boys and not standing up when the teacher spoke to me. I loved standing at the back of the class, as this gave me a full view of outside. Doves would step gently around the branches. I could see them roll their little beady eyes. I could imagine them talking to each other and I saw how they agreed, nodding their heads at the same time.

One day I was so deep in thought that I didn't hear the teacher scream my name. Everybody was looking at me but I just stood there, still in the lives of the doves. Then they started laughing at me and I had to cross my legs in fear. I could feel the trickle run; it was too late. I started to cry.

For days after this incident, girls called me names because I had wet my pants and the boys stopped talking to me, called me "Stinky" and laughed, pinching their noses closed, when I passed by their desks. This made me so angry with them I stopped making eye contact with anyone. I crept deep within myself and never smiled. At breaks at school, I would wander alone on the outskirts of the athletic field, or sit in the sun, drawing in the sand with a stick.

There were no Marmite sandwiches from Rosa to look forward to. Mrs. A would forget to pack me a snack now and again, and on these days I did not want to smell the other children's soft white bread with their whiffs of peanut butter or strawberry jam, so I steered away from them. Anyway, I dissolved into my imagination and lay back against the warm wall, baked from the winter sun. I would watch the clouds move with the wind and think up names for them. Each received an appropriate name according to its shape and form before it passed me by.

I was called into the principal's office so many times because of my daydreaming, which caused Mrs. A's handprints on my thighs, my buttocks and wherever else she could get to. This did not make me cry so much anymore, and in a strange way, it relieved me of all the pain inside my heart. I did not fear her so much now, but Masie cried for me when she discovered Mrs. A's wrath on my body. She would pull me onto her lap and say over and over how sorry she was, which I did not understand because she had done nothing to feel sorry about.

In the springtime, I discovered I could run fast. This became my life. Mrs. A joked that I can run so fast because I had these awkward, long, thin legs, like a greyhound's.

I spent afternoons after school practising, and the day arrived when the different schools competed against each other. That was the day I knew I was something, too.

The gun went off for the eighty-metres sprint for girls under nine; I shot forward, keeping my eyes on the ribbon at the end of the track. A void filled my mind and all I knew was the feel of the ribbon touching my body as I ran right through it. They applauded, all those girls who hated me; when they tried to speak to me, I just dropped my head and, with my chin on my chest, I hardly had to look into their eyes, afraid the mockery would still be evident in their faces.

And then it was time to leave the house we lived in. I knew it was my fault: I could see it in Mrs. A's eyes—for now she had to be called Mommy; well, I forgot what to call her all the time, but I saw the accusation in her eyes. We did not leave Pretoria but moved into a hotel, the Ambassador Hotel. "Mommy" had a receptionist job there now and free rooms for the three of us. It was a new adventure and I was not too sad to leave the little house with the big palm tree.

I now had to take a bus to our home/hotel from school. The teacher asked me if I was allowed to sit in the bar of the hotel and I saw the mockery in her eyes. Plus it was a trick question and I knew how to answer those.

Right in the middle of the hotel courtyard was a large fountain and a cage with black crows sitting in it, making a ruddy noise. Aunty Rose told me crows steal shiny objects; I would watch every day to see if they pinched something from one of the fancy ladies who took afternoon tea outside. I dreamt that if they found something valuable, I would in turn steal it from the crows, and I would sell it at the swap shop on my way from school. I would save up all my money and go live with my brothers.

I loved the strip of stores I passed every day, where the municipal bus dropped me after school. There was the swap shop, with everything you could imagine. The store I loved the most was the one belonging to the witch doctor. He always smiled at me as I stared through his window into his dusty store. He would gesture to me to come on in, but I knew that would just get me into trouble. Instead I would just stare at all his little bottles, boxes, tins, feathers, bones and what all, covered in a layer of dust.

One day I saw the most amazing elephant tusk lying in the window. It was large and looked so impossible that I could not resist sticking just my head into the store to ask, "Hey, is this an elephant's tooth?"

The tall, thin black man walked slowly towards the door and tilted his grey head in my direction. "That is correct, little one," he said, and then he added to his own laughter: "Imagine when he has the toothache!"

I did not catch that, because the elephant was big and therefore he could handle a larger ache, too, so proportionally it would be fine for the large elephant to handle his large pain, whether it was in his heart, head or tooth.

The black man introduced himself to me as Ndkele. I just called him "old man", "Madala". Rosa had taught me this was the respectful way to address an older man in their language. He was impressed with me and told me that when I had gathered my courage one day, I should come into the store, because there was so much he wanted to show me.

I made a plan: I had my school books ready to pile into my suitcase after the end-of-the-day bell rang at the school. I would walk slowly but surely out of the class, if I ran the teacher would call me back and then I would be totally late for the best thing of my day—visiting with my new friend, Madala.

When I was outside the school gate, I would run to the end of the street and catch the earlier bus than I was supposed to, thereby giving myself an extra half hour to spend with my new friend.

My arriving at his store and running inside caused Madala to look at me and shake his grey head. "Not so fast, not so hurried, little one—you will chase all the forefathers away with your rush."

"Sorry, Madala, but today you were going to tell me what lies in my future, remember?"

Madala was a good man; he gave me sweet white tea after he had lifted me into the high priest chair. I felt like a princess, but agreed with him that I now was the white priest of the forefathers and therefore he would not boil me up in a pot for "muti" (medicine). He laughed and winked, but he saw not a trace of fear within me at those words.

Madala said I was not afraid of the African man because I had seen too much pain in my life. I did not know what he meant, but I agreed. He asked me whom I feared more than all the mysteries and unusual surroundings in his dark, strange-smelling store. I said I had no idea what he was talking about, but for a split second I saw an arched eyebrow in my mind's eye.

Madala taught me so much about Africa, the forefathers and the healing powers of the earth. I spent every school-day afternoon with him and learnt so much about this amazing continent I lived on, Africa. Madala taught me to respect every part of nature because, he said, "nature rewards those who respect it, but hunts down the ones who trample it as insignificant under their takkies" (training shoes).

I looked at the crows in the courtyard differently and spoke soft words to them; they would tilt their heads and roll those black eyes and stop their screeching for a while. I realised I had started to have a special power over nature—if not over people, yet.

The last day I saw Madala, I did not know it was the last day. Somehow Madala knew. He took my hand in his rough, cracked, cold, black hand and told me to always respect my elders, to stay fearless and strong, and then he mumbled in a soft voice something I did not understand as he rolled his eyes way back until I saw no brown, and then he finished looking deep into my face. Tears were now running down the brown of his wrinkles. He looked sad and I knew he did not pity me, but loved me. It was strange to see the man who loved to laugh—especially at his own jokes—now crying. That was the last time I saw Madala.

We packed and Mrs. A put the furniture in storage at our new destination. I did not know where we were going and knew not to ask. I knew it had something to do with me, but Aunty Rose reassured me it would be much better than living in a hotel. I hoped so, because one Saturday evening, a wedding reception was held at the hotel. I was looking out my window onto the courtyard and saw a very young boy so drunk he could not walk. This disturbed me so much I vomited for the rest of the night.

It was a long road trip and I changed my doll's hairstyle a thousand times and napped many times before we eventually saw the sea in the distance. We ended up in a caravan park in Wilderness, called Siesta. Mrs. A told me that in this area, the cars had the registration number CAW and it stood for "cold and wet", but I thought it was the best place we ever lived.

I ran and jumped among the shrubs and wild ferns. It all looked like the scenery in the story Aunty Rose read to me about the girl in the English countryside. This was beautiful; I knew I could live in the forest forever. The caravan was nice, just like a little playhouse. I had a tiny bed which turned into a seat for the dining table in the day. The cups and saucers matched the little curtains hanging in front of the little windows. I fell in love with the place. I had carefree days and happy, solitary hours playing with imaginary pixies and fairies in the forest. Every morning when the dew was still dripping over nature, I started my quest of discovering. A day full of imagination stretched out before me. I rolled in the longer grass under majestic trees and giggled out loud, because I could not stop myself rolling down the small hills.

I was fascinated by the tadpoles I collected in an empty coffee tin, and at the end of the day, I poured them gently back into the water to find their brothers and sisters. I did not worry about fitting in with anybody, because I was by myself, with no school, no rules, and no worries. This freedom made me dizzy as I lay watching the clouds form hearts in the sky from above to me. I had this world of fairies. My little "soul flies" were all yellow and joined in with all my made-up games for the day. I would smile so much all day and only went back to the caravan to have a bite to eat. And then one day after lunch, I overheard Aunty Rose tell Mrs. A that it would be cruel to send me away.

But she did. I was being sent to George Convent, to live in the boarding school. Not only would I be away from my new world, but I would be left with non-Afrikaans-speaking children all day and all night, day after day. My world had been Afrikaans and now I would have to speak English again.

Aunty Rose gave me a Saint Christopher to hang around my neck. "It will protect you," she said, and wiped her tears.

I stood awkwardly in my new school shoes and Panama hat, both hard and stiff and a little too big: I knew it was because I was growing and Mrs. A did not want to be bothered with buying new ones again too soon. Mrs. A was complaining to the sales lady in the school uniform store about the amount of food I consumed and how fast my legs and feet were growing. I loved my long plaits and slipped my hands over the smoothness of them, one on each side of my face.

Mrs. Alexander informed me that I now had a new surname; it was like hers, Alexander. I stumbled every time the nuns asked me my name and surname. I practised like Mrs. A forced me, but still I could not pronounce it quite right and I did not remember the spelling of it. I forgot to call Mrs. A

"Mommy" and I forgot how to make the cross before and at the end of the prayers.

I was scared of the nuns. I was scared of the wooden staircase, which creaked when you walked up it by yourself. I was scared of the sea of new faces. They were all dressed exactly like me, so many of me but so different from me. I was the outsider and spoke Afrikaans. I had sweaty hands and could only fall asleep between all the other beds of girls if I held a tissue very tight in my fist. My soul flies were there, but only scarcely.

The smell of lunch was what kept me going; the soft green beans reminded me of Rosa. I had secret thoughts that she might be working in the kitchen here just to keep an eye on me.

The one thing the nuns had in common was the way they shouted my name when I would not look them in the eye. I just kept my chin glued to my chest and peeped up at them from under my lashes. That way they would never see my tears and I would avoid being hit with the ruler's metal edge on my knuckles. Here you were not allowed to cry, to talk loudly, to fight or to get excited, because it was not "ladylike".

My life was thrown into segments of time distinguished by the shrill bell. Early out of bed was the first bell telling us to get out of bed. Wash your face on the second bell. Fall onto your knees on the cold cement floor in the hallway on the third bell and pray the "Our Father" loud and strong. I did not know the words and fell asleep in the kneeling position, to be awoken by excruciating pain running through my knuckles. As I licked the blood off my hands, I cried softly and very quietly. I knew I made God so angry; the nun said so, and I was so very scared.

My days were not too difficult, though; I went to school and a tutor helped me learn English. She was very kind, a nun with a whisper of a voice, and her Afrikaans sounded so different coming from her kind expression, gentle and forgiving. She never minded me talking Afrikaans and taught me every day with such determination that I never wanted to disappoint her. I learnt fast. My pronunciation became much better, which caused this little nun to clap her hands together in approval. I felt a brand new emotion come over me: *I can.* My math was still bad, even though my counting carried over from my fingers onto the toes in my shoes. I just could not get it.

After school, we would all line up for lunch. Eating always took place in utter silence, and if you wanted to say anything, you had to lift your hand, so I never said anything and just ate every morsel off my plate. After homework, we were allowed to play outside for an hour and then received an afternoon tea with Chelsea buns. These were soft, white, sticky, sweet buns filled with raisins; you dipped them gently into the sweet white tea, slurping the liquid down. I was content because I knew my routine and tried never to be noticed for doing something too good or bad. The older girls were not too mean to me, I think because they didn't even know my name, and when one of them wanted to address me, they would call me "Boer", referring to my Afrikaans heritage. I did not mind this, because some girls came from other countries and they were called accordingly, like "Greek" or "Porra" (for Portuguese).

One day, I decided to take part in the wedding the children were playing at under the oak tree; it just looked too enticing to stay out of. I had fun and laughed and joined in and they allowed me to; they said I had good game ideas.

The next day, I decided it was time to play communion. I took the chips from the Snakes and Ladders box and placed it in a little box for the communion "wafers". I made holes in an old tin and poured it full of soft, dry sand to be used as the incense. I was the priest; all the children fell into line. I felt dignified and spoke in a dignified manner as each kneeled and received their "wafer" on the tongue. The tin was shaken for the dust to fall through like incense and I laid one "wafer" after the other on their tongues. We had so much fun, until I felt the burning eyes of Mother Superior stare into my being.

I was whipped with a long cane and sent to bed without dinner. She said I was the devil and was not to play with anyone until she decided otherwise. I trembled, not from pain or fear, but because I was the devil. That was the first of many sleepless nights. I would hear all the children breathing peacefully in their cubicles and I would hold onto my tissue as hard as I could, but still could not fall asleep. So, I decided to make up a dream world of my own. My pillow became my friend. One corner of the pillow represented me; one corner represented my future husband; the other two bottom corners of the pillow were my children, a girl and a boy. I would lie there with this family of pillow corners holding my head in their laps. I was safe and they took care of me, even though I was the devil.

My chin dropped down to my chest and I was defeated as the children teased me for peeing in the bed. I became "Stinky" again and they forgot how much they had enjoyed my games.

*   *   *

The train just clicked and clicked, annoying me. It made me stand up and stride into the passage. Two people were standing, kissing, at the end of the coach, and a man was blowing his cigarette smoke out of the open window, leaning so far out I wondered what he was looking at.

"Hullo, sweetie," he said, looking straight into my face.

He had approached me without my noticing. I was startled: "I'm not your fucking sweetie."

I felt how he staggered backwards a step and I stormed back into my compartment and latched the door. I felt so dirty and angry when this type of disgusting man approached me with his sly, eager lust in his eyes; I could kill them.

CHAPTER SIX

A Child of Jesus

I remembered how we went off to the sea with the convent, all the way from George to Betty's Bay. It was a bright, sunny day. The nuns were in a good mood. The children whose parents were too far away, a bunch of us, had to stay in the convent over weekends. Mrs. A did not live so far away, but she might have forgotten about me here. The bus driver winked at me in the rear-view mirror and turned the transistor radio up; the sweet sound and rhythm of "Downtown" was sung by Petula Clark and I swayed to the beat.

We all received our swimming costumes and a towel and off we raced for a day in the sun and sea. I discovered bluebottles: little sea creatures that were blown up like tiny balloons, but with a long tail that stung the living daylights out of you. The nuns would rub our sting marks with mentholated spirits and send us back to play.

I looked at the nuns sitting huddled under a big Coca Cola umbrella; they resembled a group of penguins. I giggled at the thought. Because I was the devil I knew I would never become a nun, and somehow felt relieved, since you were not allowed to take off your nun-outfit on the beach and that did not seem like fun at all.

The nuns spoke to me differently after the "communion" episode. I knew they were making plans to change me from being the devil. I was their mission now: they would convert this Afrikaans devil. They watched me carefully, but I saw them; I saw the nun squinting her eyes as I rocked to the music on the bus.

At the end of the school year, you could touch the excitement of the long summer vacation. The girls and nuns were all in good moods and spoke of their plans for this stretch of leisure ahead. My soft-spoken elocution nun was going to Italy, and instead of teaching me any English, she began leading me geographically through the fascinating continent of Europe. She trailed her little white finger along the map, explaining how her travels would take her to her favourite destination, Rome and the Vatican City, the capital of all Roman Catholics. I was amazed at the size of this religion. She explained about the Pope and I saw an angelic expression on her face. She wiped a little tear from her cheek and smiled, so happy. I knew what she meant; I had this feeling when I lay in the green folds of Wilderness.

All our suitcases were packed and we were allowed to sit on them or the steps outside, waiting for our parents, drivers or relatives to pick us up. The girls were chattering like thousands of little, excited birds, laughing as one by one they were called by their surname when their lift arrived; hurried goodbyes were shouted as they disappeared into summer. I sat and sat and sat and was the last one, as the only girl who waited with me walked off with her driver. He had such shiny shoes. All I could think was that I was going to stay in this rotten place the entire summer.

The nun brought me a stale Chelsea bun and tea. I was wondering what they would feed me, since all the food had to be finished at the end of the year. The shadows under the big trees started stretching into thin skeletons, becoming vague, and then I was called inside, with the click of tongues because it was getting dark. I sat in the foyer on the only bench, hard and wooden; it was solely for those who had done something to deserve being called to Mother Superior's office. I did not want to sit here. I did not even have the comfort of my pillow to hold onto; what would happen to me?

The trees outside grew and grew, stretching their tentacles into the foyer; the leaves tickled me under my arms. I climbed onto the branches and hopped like a squirrel; I gathered acorns with the local squirrels and they taught me to speak squirrel. They showed me how to gather acorns and how to hide them for winter when there would be no food. The grumble of my tummy woke me, and then I saw the nun unlocking the front door, and there stood Mrs. A.

In the car was a boy, Mrs. A's son, Roy. He had on his high school blazer; he looked about fourteen years old. I stared at him and he gave me a skew smile and looked away. That was the most acknowledgement he gave me the entire summer.

We all had to fit and find our little space in the caravan, but I did not mind sleeping on the top stretcher overhead. My days were filled with trying to recapture my initial love for this forest, but the caravan park was filled with so many other people it was hard to find my fairies.

I complained to Aunty Rose that my fairies had all gone; she took my hands in hers and told me to hold onto moments and enjoy them as if they would never return again.

"Judy, when you find or experience something you love, even just the moment looking at a butterfly, enjoy it and place it deep in your heart—that moment may never return again."

Mrs. A went to a tent Christian revival gathering. It was within walking distance from the caravan and I watched her walking away with her shoulders slumped; she did not "float" when she walked anymore. I sat on the canvas chair for a long time, waiting for her to return. I saw her silhouette returning at dusk; it seemed like she had a little hop in her step on her way back. She said she was saved, but I could not make out from what.

The next night, Aunty Rose and Mrs. A went off together to the revival tent. They returned with mascara streaks under their eyes and they were laughing and smiling a lot. They started sitting in little groups with neighbouring caravan dwellers, singing songs while clapping their hands, swaying their arms in the air and crying a whole lot. They stared into space, looking a bit like my angelic nun. Roy laughed at both his mother and Aunty Rose and I heard him telling them they were now in a cult. I admired Roy for the way he was never scared of his mother and told her just what he thought. I would cheer him on in my mind even when I did not agree with him.

The night came when Mrs. A forced me to go to the tent revival with her. I was so scared because Roy shouted after his mother that it was not right to force Jesus on a child.

She stood dead still, turned on her heel and looked back at him. "I will do with her as I wish. Anything is better than what she had with her pathetic parents!"

With this, she grabbed my hand, and off we went so I could become a reborn Christian.

The whole thing passed me by in a strange haze of people shouting in a language that was neither Afrikaans nor English. I decided the people were from Italy, the Vatican City with all the Christians. The next moment, I felt Mrs. A's nail in my back as she pushed me to go forward. I asked her what to do; she said I should lay my sins at the foot of Jesus. I stood in a long line and waited my turn—turn for what, I was not sure.

When the pastor looked at me, he gave me a gentle nudge and asked if I had any sins, to which I replied quickly, before I lost my courage: "I am the devil. I chew my nails and wet my pants."

The pastor wrapped his whole hand over my forehead and with one push, he shouted, "In the name of Jesus…"

The rest I did not hear because he threw me right flat onto my back. I scrambled up, but this fat lady pressed me down to the floor. All I could see was her greasy grey hair parted in the wrong place on her head. I wanted to re-part it, but it was too dirty looking.

Mrs. A and Rose took me around to all the vacationers and declared me reborn, upon which they all started hugging me and made me sing with them.

Aunty Rose went to pick mushrooms in the forest for dinner. We walked into the caravan to the most delicious smell I had ever experienced. Mrs. A warned Rose not to pick mushrooms because she did not know the poisonous ones. Aunty Rose just laughed and made us pray over these delicately evil little mushrooms; also, just in case we all died in the night, she prayed for our souls.

I could not fall asleep and kept thinking how they would discover us dead in our beds the next day. I parted my hair precisely in the middle of my head and tried to curl the ends a little, and since I was now a Christian, I folded my hands into the prayer position on my chest so this was how they would find me the next day. I waited for death and fell asleep.

The next day, I believed in Jesus with all my heart. I sang all the songs with fellow believers, and as I washed our plates at the communal block, I smiled at everybody washing their dishes beside me. Roy called me a Jesus freak and I did not care; Jesus had kept me alive after eating those poisonous mushrooms and that was all that counted.

I was not looking forward to going back to those nuns, but excited they would not see me as the devil anymore. But I never returned to the convent.

CHAPTER SEVEN

Hell

I packed my suitcase and left with Roy and Mrs. A for my new school. This time we drove very, very far. I wondered if it was going to be an English or Afrikaans school.

It was an Afrikaans one, and in the most remote town I'd ever seen: Middelburg, Transvaal. The boarding school was painted a sad blue, like those days when the sun just does not seem to be able to push through those stubborn grey clouds. The hostel was painted an even sadder kind of green, the green you would find in a mental hospital. I saw this colour in the place when we fetched my mother after she had had a nervous breakdown. This was no good omen.

Mrs. A looked at me for a long time as she said goodbye. "Judy, you have to be brave and strong and hold your head high."

"I promise, Mummy." That was what she wanted me to call her; it was pronounced different from "Mammie" in Afrikaans, so it was okay. She was my English Mummy. My Afrikaans Mammie—well, I had no idea.

Mrs. A tilted her head to one side and her hair fell over. She had a cow's lick and said it was the only thing she and I had in common. I loved her so much and was glad we shared this. Her eyes were full of tears; I did not understand why— we had said goodbye many times before and she had taught me never to cry when we parted.

I frowned and asked her, "What is my surname here?"

Mrs. A blinked her eyes and grabbed her hanky out of her handbag. Her eyebrow flew into its familiar arch. "What the hell do you mean? You know you're Alexander. Dammit,

Judy, will you ever learn that I'm doing the best I can for you? You know very well I saved you from the pits." She lowered her voice to a whisper. "You could be sleeping with the pigs if I hadn't saved you from those pathetic parents of yours!"

At this point I could hardly hear her, but I knew the words off by heart, anyway.

I turned away from her frown and dropped my chin. "I know, Mummy."

Roy looked at us through the car window and waved at me. I lifted a wilted hand and felt my tears coming, so I dropped my chin a little lower. Mrs. A saw this and told me to look her in the eyes.

She warned me she would not be able to visit me so often because it was far away, but the school had her phone number if they needed it. She needed to take Roy to his school and said a hurried goodbye. She turned on her heel, walking away in her navy suit, her stockings making their familiar swoosh sound as she floated off. Some of the girls sitting under the tree looked at me and decided I was boring, so they just continued with their own conversation.

I didn't know how long I stood looking at the dust settling over the dirt road as the Mercedes sped off. The sound of a shrill bell shook me back to reality.

This place had no lush, big green trees like in Wilderness; it was not green at all, but brown. I was in Middelburg, Transvaal. Everything was covered in a brown-grey dust. There were only a few trees and even they weren't eye-hurting green; just that covered-in-dust colour.

As I walked into the sleeping quarters, I heard the Afrikaans bursting out of all the girls' mouths. They were loud, all speaking at the same time. I could understand them perfectly; the pitch ranges in their voices were totally familiar. I knew the meaning of the twists and turns their voices took. Without looking at them as they spoke, I knew instinctively when something was a question or a statement—I even knew when their mouths were smiling as they said something. It is a dramatic language and the laughter was not subdued. These girls would have a tough time in a convent, I thought. As loud as they had been, just as abruptly, everyone fell silent, and then in one choir voice, they greeted the matron as she walked into the room. "Goeie naand, Mev. Scheepers!" ("Good evening, Mrs. Scheepers!")

She wanted to see the new kids in her office. I stood in expectation of rules and regulations with the other new ones, all of us eyeing each other. I knew that look; they sized you up and tried to place you into a box. *What and who are you? Are you from a nearby farm with rich, wholesome parents, a nervous kid whose parents think the independence of a boarding school life will bring you out of your skin, or are you the child whose parents live in some rural area and no good schools are available there?* I had my own scenario and needed to keep the true story hidden. I now knew we were running from my biological parents. The story I told was that my mother was the supervisor of a chain group and had to travel to all the cities in South Africa to visit them, and she had placed me somewhere central so she could see me more often. I knew this would not backfire when she did not make it; it was just because she was so important in her job.

The matron talked loudly and seriously about all the different punishments for the different violations of the school rules. It sounded very severe and I realised you could get spanked for anything at any time by these fat, strong white arms. I would rather have died, and made an oath to never do anything wrong. In my mind's eye I saw one of those pamphlets the tent church had given me; it depicted the road to heaven as a hard, narrow path with many stumbling blocks. I wondered why I should walk this hard path, anyhow. Then you saw the end of the two trails and the hard path ended in heaven and the other, easy road stopped abruptly and then you fell into a chorus of flames, devils and demons and funny-looking goats all around you. Well, that must have been the hard path I was on right now, but the end should then be safely in heaven.

The whole group and the matron were looking at me. I realised I had missed the question. "Pardon?" I squeaked.

The matron squinted her eyes as she asked in deliberate, clear Afrikaans: "Is it more interesting outside than what I am saying?"

"No, Mrs...umm...excuse me." I flushed and crossed my legs and wanted the earth to swallow me. What would my punishment be for dreaming instead of listening?

The matron excused everyone and asked me to stay behind. I felt my heart miss its familiar beats; my chest closed with fear and the loud throbbing in my ears became deafening. The matron made me sit next to her on the couch and told me in no uncertain manner that she could see right through me, and if I thought I was superior to anyone, she would personally break my little will. Also, due to the lice infestation, I would have to have my long hair cut short within the next few days.

I cradled my head in my pillow that night and felt warm tears wet my cheeks. Masie had taught me that a woman's pride was her hair and I brushed it with a hundred strokes each night to let it grow. Among all the breathing bodies around me, I could hear the soft sniffing of a homesick girl. Oh, I wished I only had homesickness. Who would I be longing for—Rosa, my little black crow who smelt like custard and Vicks at the same time? Aunty Rose, who reminded me, as she said goodbye, that I was God's child and He was everywhere? Madala, who had become my protective witch doctor, or my biological mother and father and my two brothers? I didn't know.

I was still exhausted the next day as the wake-up bell rang in my ears. It was the matron; she walked around with the hand bell, ringing it in the ears of all those who did not jump out of bed.

The school uniform was green. That was what you saw in the school hall in assembly: a sea of green. The principal was a large man who snorted between his sentences. I had trouble following him. He spoke about the Voortrekker wagon we had to push or pull up the hill. He said that the view would be good, and because we were strong Afrikaners, we could and must do it. He made us all look at the back wall of the hall. There were pictures of our State President, our ministers and some angry-looking ancestors. He said we had to push this wagon up the hill in these people's honour. We had to study, be diligent and see that we excelled on the sport fields.

Proudly these Afrikaner children sang the South African anthem, "Uit die blou van onse hemel" ("Ringing out from our blue heavens"), and then the school anthem. The dominee (Afrikaans church clergyman) said his prayer long and loudly: he prayed for the white Afrikaner, that we would be strong and courageous and win our war. I wondered why he sounded so angry and what war we were entering. I avoided looking at the photographs of those angry men hanging in the back of the hall at every assembly.

Walking to the hostel after school became my favourite time of the day. I stopped to look at the ants running in their little rows—looking for water, I was sure. Middelburg was in the midst of a terrible drought and had a severe water shortage; one of the things we had to pray for was rain, every day. The dominee said we had made God angry and therefore we had brought this drought upon ourselves. He said God would not lift His hand to replenish the water supplies until we sought His face. I did not understand this, but at night, lying close in my pillow, I would look out the window into the cloudless sky and try to seek God's face. I actually saw it once, too. If I took the stars and outlined them in a certain way, I could see His face clearly. I think I saw Him wink at me; it made me smile and fall asleep without having to clench my tissue in my hand too stiffly.

Upon waking the next morning, I saw it was raining. You could smell the wet earth. It was Saturday and most girls had gone home for the weekend. After breakfast, we had to wash our hair and then we were free for the rest of the morning. It was still raining softly outside when the matron snipped off my long hair. I bit my lip until it bled and did not cry. I stood in front of the mirror and looked into my face. I saw my little soul flies all over the mirror, flying around my face; the colours of the rainbow were over my head. I tried to shake them away, but they lingered and tried to lift my spirits. I heard the matron's squeaky brown shoes disappear down the hall. I walked outside into the rain, my bare feet stomping into the mud puddles and, letting the water run over my face, I looked up into the sky and pretended to sacrifice my hair to the rain god. I ran and danced and felt the water splash up my legs. I could hear nothing but tasted the water and smelt the drops flirting with my salty tears. I didn't know how long I was out in the rain but went inside only when it stopped. I turned back and looked over at a koppie in the far distance; a beautiful rainbow hung in the purple sky.

The matron was standing in the foyer as I walked by. She held out a towel for me. She cleared her throat and said, "You'll get used to the short hair."

I did not recognise my voice as I felt my eyes turn cold. "No, I will never."

At this stage of my life, I knew with total certainty that I hated schoolwork, no matter in which language it was. I found my true love outside on the sports grounds. I took part in all the track and field events, from long jump to high jump. I loved the javelin. On the track, I ran the one hundred and two hundred metres in the school's record time and the coach, who was also my Afrikaans teacher, decided it was time to fully exploit my talents for the good of the school and "Afrikaner Dom".

In the mornings, we got up at six a.m., but I rose at five with a shake from a fellow athlete and we would go running for an hour. I heard the soft drop of my feet on the ground as my breath rose in a rhythm with my heart. I felt the wind on my face as I paced my steps. I felt alive and in control and needed to go faster and faster, usually outrunning my partner, but neither she nor I cared. I would feel sad as I climbed under the shower after the run and let my tears flow quietly with the water: the best of the day was now over and I had nothing to look forward to at school except ridicule and unmotivated reprimanding. It was only in the afternoons I would be able to escape into the world of athletics again.

The food in the hostel was quite bad, but my hunger caused me to eat faster and just listen to the complaints of the other girls as they pushed their plates away. I knew they would be able to eat their tuck shop snacks later, but I had no part of that; I never had any money. The girls would sit in a little confidential circle on their beds as they munched on their snacks, big cake tins filled to the brim with anything edible, talking with lollipops in their mouths until the red saliva juices would trickle out of the corners of their mouths and they would catch me staring; they would burst into a choir of laughter as I scrambled out the door. "Weirdo!" they would shout after me, and as I stood in the hallway, I could still hear them speaking about me. I was called the skinny kid with the fish eyes who always looked hungry and sad. The only thing I did right was that I could run fast, and then they burst into laughter again as they speculated I must have learnt running due to hunger which got me chasing after the veggie man's delivery cart.

I stood, shaking, and as before, I felt hatred well up inside me. I became angry with Mrs. A for never coming for me, for not giving me any money. I was angry with my mother who had just given me away. I was angry because of my situation and being among people who thought I was weird because I spoke so little.

I ran to the bathroom to look at my reflection in the mirror and I saw these large blue eyes looking back at me. I lifted my skirt and looked at my thin white legs and the knobby knees and knew the girls were right: I was an awkward-looking thing. My short blonde hair was hardly brushed and I don't remember if I ever washed behind my ears as Aunty Rose had taught me, but it was the drought and we had to bathe in someone else's bathwater every night, and I hated that even more than being dirty, so in the evenings I would just wash my feet in the dirty bathwater and in the mornings I showered so fast I never gave my body a second thought.

It was the athletic season and I spent every free moment on the athletic field with no complaints from the matron. The running took my mind off things, and as the coach pushed his thumb on the button of the stopwatch, he smiled and became excited until I smiled, too. I realised I was doing something really good. The coach explained that I needed to acknowledge I would be representing our school at the inter-school competitions and should keep it up. He brought me three bananas at the field every day and sat happily as I munched each banana.

With another cloudless sky, the day arrived for the school athletics. The children walked in rows, fitting perfectly next to each other in the pavilion. They began singing their songs to inspire the teams and became louder as they competed in their cries for victory. There were three teams, red, yellow and green. I had a green bow pinned on my shirt to show which team I was in.

I waited for the gun.

"On your marks, get set—" *Boom!*

I sprinted like never before, then I heard the yelling of the children and, out of the corner of my eye, I saw the green team on their feet and knew they were cheering for me. I accelerated and felt the ribbon as I flew through the finish line. My heart was racing as I looked up at the green team going berserk. I could not believe my eyes; I had done it, and I had caused this.

After I had given my name and received the time, I walked over to the crowd of children. They patted me on the back and shouted "well done!" over and over. I felt something within me I had never experienced. I became quiet among the noise and looked at my weird long legs and knobby knees and knew they had done it.

I did this five times that day and experienced the acknowledgement from the green team five times. My head was spinning and I felt light headed; I felt so good.

I fell asleep peeping at the little trophy next to me on the bedside table. It glistened in the moonlight. I sighed and dreamt I was riding the whitest horse over soft green meadows, and then my brothers were there too, smiling and laughing with their blonde hair blowing in the soft breeze.

I practised every day until the inter-school athletics took place. Once again I succeeded in making my coach proud. He told me so, over and over. He also called me his little running machine.

Then the athletic season was over and the days became shorter and the mornings ice cold as we climbed out of our beds. There was no heating in the hostel, but the coal stoves in the classrooms were a blessing, and everybody tried to sit nearest them. I became very hungry again and wondered if I would ever get enough food.

The morning I found worms in my porridge, I thought I was going to die. The other girls pushed their plates away, knowing they would have to eat their tuck shop treats earlier that day. The matron told us that the worms were due to the drought and the maize was the way it was and we had to eat it or go hungry. I could not do it; I could not eat this and, in fact, I was scared of worms. At night I dreamt of the worms crawling in my stomach and I would wake to grumbles in my tummy. During break at school, I would sneak into the classroom to see if some kid had discarded her sandwiches in the dustbin. I found sandwiches in the girls' restroom. The bigger girls were more interested in sneaking in a quick smoke at break than eating their snack. I would grab it out of the dustbin as the bell rang and everybody left the bathroom. I stuffed the food down my throat without tasting anything and gulped some water from the tap to help it go down. One day this caused me to be late for class and I smelt like cigarette smoke from the bathroom. I was sent to the principal, whose wrath was great. My punishment would be to do long-distance running in the afternoons and the coach was called in to make sure she understood to place a hell of an amount of pressure on me.

I reported to the field in the afternoon. The long-distance coach was a fat, mean-looking woman with bleached hair which did not move in the wind. She gave me a gruelling schedule and held her whipping cane tightly in her hand, ready to use as I passed her on the track. She held her stopwatch in her hand but I knew she was not using it; she would make up times and shout them into my face.

All the victory and acknowledgement of my previous successes decreased and then totally disappeared as the kids forgot how much pride I had brought with all my winning on the sport field. Slowly they forgot and the ridicule started again. I was nobody once more.

One evening, one of the girls declared somebody had stolen her money. The matron's brown shoes squeaked angrily over the floors as she went to each person to ask if they had taken it. I knew she loved this blonde girl, and her parents even more; her father was a prominent lawyer in town and her mother played the church organ.

This was outrageous. The matron said she would find the culprit. She walked to each dorm room and selected the poor kids to go to the dining hall. The rich kids would not steal, since they had enough. So we stood in a row with the matron walking up and down past us, explaining non-stop the severity of stealing. She would hold up the Bible and read the Ten Commandments and sway her whipping cane in front of our faces. None of us spoke. It seemed like ages before she eventually asked the thief to step forward. No one moved. She started all over again, telling us how we would all end up in jail, shouting how pathetic we were. I looked over to see who was standing in shame with me. Everybody had their heads dropped, so I dropped my chin onto my chest, my favourite position.

Matron asked the thief to step forward. Nobody moved. It became late. She switched the lights off. She squeaked past us and started to pray in a loud, moaning voice; she pleaded to God to show her who it was and softly whispered that the thief should now step forward. No one moved. She explained that we would all end up in hell, and then some of the senior girls entered the dining hall, emphasising the same matter as Matron went to wash her face and drink some water. I was just as thirsty and could imagine the cold water running down Matron's throat. Then we were asked to please step forward if we were the one who had taken the money or knew who it was.

There was a faint shuffle to my right. The lights were switched on; it blinded me for a moment, and then I saw that this girl was gesturing towards me—she thought I had taken the money. My head shot up and I said it was not true.

So, the lights went off again and the matron returned and the interrogation began all over again. I became so tired I felt like sleeping in the standing position. The next moment, my knees wobbled and I thought I was going to faint; the lights shot on and Matron asked if I wanted to admit to anything. I shook my head and the lights went off. That was when the matron started speaking, basically just to me, about how freeing it would be for me to admit it; how sad it was to keep all these innocent girls standing here. I was basically punishing them for my sins. Then she started to describe heaven, how beautiful it would be in the end, and I saw the picture of the two paths in my mind—the easy and the hard. This, the hard one I was on, would eventually lead me to eternal rest, peace and, I was so sure, food. I knew I had not taken this money, but I stepped forward.

My legs were swollen from the whipping, but the scorn of all the girls hurt even more. I was shunned. I could feel they locked everything. When I was around or walked into the room, the loud talking would turn into whispers. I was once again the outcast, with a new name added to my repertoire: thief!

One morning, I woke up with a sore throat and a throbbing head. The nurse gave me an Aspirin and sent me off to school. I was hot and my head became so sore I went to excuse myself from the long-distance running in the afternoon. The coach stood like a statue in front of me and said she knew all the tricks in the book about how to get out of training, and that I could stop if I fell dead on the track. I started running, my head bouncing up and down, sending sharp pains down my spine. All I could see were the droplets on my eyelashes glistening in the sun; I could not see the track. I concentrated on the teardrops falling from my eyes.

I started coughing and slowed down, and that was when I felt the whip on the back of my legs. The witch was behind me and I could swear I even saw movement in her stiff blonde hairdo, and then nothing made sense as the sky circled over my head and the singing in my ears deafened the cries of kids around me.

Mrs. A was standing next to the hospital bed when I came to. She looked so angry and I expected her to tell me what a terrible person I was, but instead she smiled and told me she was taking me out of this hellhole of a school.

*   *   *

The monotonous sound of the train had lulled me to sleep, but now we had stopped and I knew we were in Kroonstad in the middle of the night. The train always stopped here at around one in the morning. I felt thirsty and stepped outside the compartment to see if the vendors were walking around, selling snacks and drinks. The air was crisp outside. A toothless black woman smiled at me. I bought a bottle of soda and a packet of chips. She untied knot upon knot of her handkerchief to give me my change, and when I saw her little arthritic hands, she reminded me of Rosa. I told her to keep the change. I went back to sit in the compartment and prayed that nobody would be joining me in this solitary ride to freedom.

My wish did not come true; this old lady shuffled inside and asked me to place her suitcase in the overhead space. I did it without a smile—*do not get too close*—as this was my solitary ride and I wanted no conversation of any kind. Her bedding was delivered and I helped her make up her bench, and after she had tied a scarf around her freshly curled grey hair, she went to sleep.

I sat in the dark and smelt the mothballs coming from the intruder. I wondered why old people always smelt as if they had been preserved. What would I remember when I was old and grey? I hoped better things than life had dealt me so far. My thoughts went to the pillow. I would have a husband and two children, a boy and a girl. I would live in a nice house and take care that the house shone, and the children would be hugged and smell of roses. First I had to get that interview with South African Airways. I had to get a job and meet the person who would deliver me from life's evil and we would live happily forever after.

CHAPTER EIGHT

Life in the Kruger National Park

I looked out of the window of the Mercedes as we sped away from Middelburg. We left a dust streak in the air. I did not even look back; I could not look back. I lay back on the backseat of the car, not feeling too well yet but safe and secure. Mrs. A stopped at the Wimpy Bar for breakfast. I was so happy to sit with all that bacon and egg in front of me, but I found myself still too ill to eat. Sadly, I lay in the back on the pillows as we went on with our trip, sucking on cold grapes and nibbling small pieces of crackers, since that was all my body could digest without ejecting it.

As we travelled into the Lowveld, I felt my body coming slowly to life. We drove past towns I had never heard of: Belfast, and then Waterval Boven, then Nelspruit. In Nelspruit, Mrs A bought me a "Gluck", a lime-green troll with long hair and a little brush. I loved it.

We had lunch and next came White River, a lush and beautiful little town. I became intensely aware of my surroundings: the abundant green plants alongside the road. Barberton daisies fought for their spot in the sun, of which there seemed to be plenty. Sun was shining between the tall pine trees in spurts and sparkling in intervals on my face as I stared out at the surroundings through the car window.

I sighed and Mrs. A asked if I was okay. I answered, with the feel of the sun on my face and my eyes catching glimpses of my soul flies around me, "I think I'm going to love it here. Is it far to where we are going to live?"

"Yes, you're going to love it here. We're living in the Kruger National Park. I'm the receptionist in the Pretoriuskop Camp and we have a house there. We have to get there before the main gate closes because they don't allow vehicles into the Park after five p.m."

I sat forward and asked, with astonishing pulses running through my head, "Are we going to live with wild animals?"

"Yes, and it's a beautiful life—you'll see wild animals are the best neighbours you could ever wish for."

Mrs. A looked happy to give me the details, telling me we were fenced in, so most animals were outside our camp. Pretoriuskop takes its name from the nearby kopje (hill) where Voortrekker Willem Pretorius, a member of Carl Trichardt's 1848 expedition to Delagoa Bay, is buried.

I sat staring out of the window even more intently. I was feeling so excited about this new adventure. I did not know my own likes and dislikes too much yet, but I had found I loved the Wilderness and its nature, and this might be a little like that. Wow, I was going to see animals every day. Monkeys would make me smile every day. I knew this was going to be special and my soul flies all came dancing around my head in circles. I knew they were smiling, too. I just wondered if Aunty Rose was already there, or if she was even joining us at all.

Along the way, we saw baboons in the road and had to slow down for them to pass first. Mrs. A explained that I should always remember that we, as people, had come into the animals' world and should always respect them. As we drove past, I bowed to the red backsides they turned on us and Mrs. A laughed out loud. I felt happy.

We went through Numbi Gate into the Kruger National Park; the guard smiled as he let us through. I felt like royalty, hearing him call Mrs. A's name and wishing her a beautiful evening! She signed the register and he asked if I was the "Piekanienie" (little one). We drove very slowly; the speed limit was fifteen miles per hour because this was animal country and we had to respect them. I stretched my eyes to see the first wild animal, which would become my favourite animal for the rest of my life.

We only had five miles to go to Pretoriuskop and Mrs. A made a small detour to a waterhole. There, the next moment, plopped the biggest nostrils out of the water, and that was when I saw on the embankment near the car a mommy hippo wobbling fatly alongside her baby hippo. My heart skipped a beat; they were so close and so beautifully strange.

Mrs. A spoke in a whisper. "This is the most dangerous animal in the world." I could not believe it; the mommy hippo seemed to have a smile. The baby followed its mother ever so closely. "They don't fear humans," she told me, and I wished this fearlessness for myself.

I sat staring at these majestic animals and decided, yes, this was it, they would be my favourite animal for the rest of my life and I would like to learn more about them.

We drove up to the wooden gate of Pretoriuskop. Another white smile in a black face opened the gate and saluted Mrs. A. She waved her gold-bangled arm at him, and then I saw her pop some money into his hand, upon which he smiled even bigger and, very erect, he saluted us through, winking at me.

Bungalows stood all over with their neat thatched roofs. We drove to one off the road, the employees' accommodation. These were neat bungalows, too, only larger; more in the shape of a house. I felt excited as I walked into the cool foyer. The floors were shiny concrete and the smell of Cobra wax polish mixed with the grass roof filled my nose.

I loved everything about my new home. I ran down the corridor to find my room. Mrs. A shouted it was the second on the left. I stood dead still and then rubbed my hand over the bed cover with all the animals on it. The curtains had the same print. When I drew them open, I saw rows and rows of mango trees and a very large garden with a high fence at the end. Then I saw the blue monkeys in the trees and gave a

shriek of excitement. I looked around and saw approval in
Mrs. A's eyes. I ran to her and hugged her around the waist
and felt so good.

I had found my most favourite place in the entire world. I ran
back to the window and told her to look at the monkeys
jumping playfully from branch to branch.

The house was large for just Mrs. A and me. It seemed
Aunty Rose was not joining us here. I dared not ask because
I had learnt never to ask her tricky questions, since she might
explode. In time I would find out, anyhow.

I found a young black girl in the kitchen, cooking dinner.
Mrs. A introduced us. Her name was Joyful, but she looked
very sad to me. She did not look into my eyes and I knew it
was not because she was shy.

Mrs A tasted the minced beef she was cooking and gave a
disapproving grunt. She added some spices. I asked to go
outside. I was told to slam the screen door first to chase the
baboons out of the trees, because they could be dangerous; to
stand still when I saw a snake; and not to try and touch a
blue-headed lizard. Mrs. A said that was enough information
for starters and I walked out the back door, slamming the
screen door hard. Mrs. A shouted from the kitchen, "Don't
break the bloody thing, just a slam!"

I shrugged my shoulders and stepped out slowly towards the
trees, forgetting to look out for snakes. Fat mangoes hung all
over the trees. I wished to eat some, thinking of Adam and
Eve. I was going to have some fun games in this backyard
with a food source at my disposal at all times.

I was called in for dinner. Mrs. A played opera music on the
record player. She sipped on her gin and tonic and told me
the story of *Madame Butterfly*. The opera singer sang
beautifully and I danced down the passage to take my bath;
my imagination was running wild as I soaked in the water,
dreaming of living here for the rest of my life.

It was pitch, pitch dark when I switched the light off. I walked with my hands stretched out to find my bed, kneeled in front of it and begged God to let me live here forever. As I was still praying, I heard, over the sound of crickets, frogs, night owls, and other nightlife, the roar of a lion. Nobody had ever told me what it sounded like, but I knew instinctively. I ran to the window, opening the window wider to hear better; I climbed onto the large ledge to sit and listen. Mrs. A popped in to say goodnight and told me not to stay on the ledge too long.

The lion sounded sad. I spoke to him softly. I encouraged him, saying it was not that bad, and he needed to rest so he could find food tomorrow. I stared at the thousands of stars and realised I'd never seen the sky so crowded with stippling shimmers. It looked like a mess to me, such a busy sky over here.

The bark of the monkeys woke me early and I could not wait for the sun to come out, so I dressed and stepped into my new world. I was going to explore every inch of the wild and learn as much as I could about the animals.

I walked to the gate where we had come into the camp. The same gateman greeted me with his white smile. "Aikona!" he said. "You cannot walk out the gate!"

I told him I was not stupid, upon which he started laughing and polishing his already shiny brown shoes. He spoke to me in Afrikaans and said he had thought I was some ignorant tourist and that I wouldn't believe what they got up to: packing picnics ready for a walk outside the gate, not realising this was not the zoo; these were real animals. I told him zoo animals were real too, but he disagreed, since they were fenced in and did not have their usual or normal personalities, because the wild animals see movement as their meal and the zoo animals see movement as the bringer of the meal. At that, he started to click his tongue over and over. He believed if you opened all the zoo gates, the animals would not leave, because they had lost their souls.

"When you are locked up, you lose your soul," he repeated.

I told him his shoes shone nicely and he smiled and waved as I walked off. I came home to the smell of bacon and eggs and felt good enough to eat again. Mrs. A's shift at the reception office started at one p.m. and I was to keep myself busy and not wander too far away and be back for lunch; Joyful would have food made for me and Mrs. A was having lunch at the restaurant and a staff meeting.

My days were mine and I explored. Evenings, Mrs. A and I would have dinner together and she would play records to me and teach me about music. She loved one particular record, a group of concertinas called "Siesta". The other music she taught me was opera; she made me listen carefully until I could distinguish between violins and cellos. All the time, Mrs. A's eyes seemed sad and tired. She was sipping on her drink every night and sighing a lot.

I, on the other hand, was happy. I filled my days sitting on the edge of our garden, looking deep into the bush to see wild animals from up close. If I stayed motionless, they came close, and I could stare at the eyelashes of the zebra, the slow grazing of the impala. I would throw my fruit peels over the fence in the hope of enticing the plant-eating animals nearer. I begged Mrs. A to take me for a ride out of the gate to see more animals, but she just complained that she was too tired.

One morning, Mrs. A told me to come up to the reception bungalow. She introduced me to the game warden, Mr. Retief Cilliers, a lank, friendly-looking man who smiled until little cracks formed at the corners of his blue eyes. This man became an integral part of my life. Every morning at sunrise, I would be ready and waiting for the arrival of his Land Rover. I would jump in the back with his daughter, Letitia.

She was about eleven years old, a year and a half older than me. She was the epitome of the beauty and composure I wished for myself. I copied everything she did exactly. Her long, thin, platinum-blonde hair had a natural flip at the end of the ponytail; I would roll the end of my very short ponytail around an empty toilet roll, but to no avail—my thick, blonde hair would just curl in all directions and make my whole face look baby-like, not smooth and sophisticated like Letitia's.

This girl was soft spoken and had knowledge of every animal. Her father would quiz her as we drove into the bush, on no particular road but right among the bushes and long grass, swerving every now and again for some big rock, anthill or broken tree stump, which caused us to fall over on the backseat and burst into laughter.

Mr. Cilliers would hush us; "You two monkeys there at the back will chase all the animals away with those giggles, and then we'll see nothing today!" Mr. Cilliers had a black game ranger, called Piet, in the front seat, and on hearing us being called monkeys, he laughed too.

We would approach the drinking holes in utter silence and stare, with soft whispers of, "Look," pointing our fingers in the direction of "our" find. An elephant began to step slowly and cautiously into the water, placing one foot with effort in front of the other until he was submerged in the water up to his belly. This was when the rest of the elephants began to walk closer; quite a few appeared from behind the wild fig and Jackal berry trees. They sprayed muddy water over their bodies. I stared and needed to pinch myself to make sure I was not dreaming. They were so peaceful and undisturbed. The little trunks of the young ones were working deliberately, sucking water and spraying it over their backs. I detected a smile on their faces and the sounds of enjoyment filled the warm sunshine. The birds busied themselves with the noisy building of nests.

Piet, the assistant game ranger, pointed to a green stripe sliding up a tree not far from our open Land Rover. "Boomslang," he whispered and looked into my eyes for a sign of fear, but I showed none. "I see," was all I said and watched it glide effortlessly up the rough bark of the tree.

As we drove away, Mr. Cilliers explained that that snake had quite a few varied colours. They could be leaf green, like the one we had just seen, or bright green, or even black with dark grey and black-edged belly scales; there were also brick-red to rust-red ones, with orange-pink bellies.

I asked my first question: "How will you know the different snakes from each other in order to receive the correct anti-venom if they bite you?"

Mr. Cilliers looked at me in amazement. "Okay, Judy, we have a deal—I'll give you a book and you study the snakes I've marked in this book, and I promise you, you'll never receive the wrong anti-venom. You'll also be sure to check what the snake that bites you looks like and identify it within minutes, deal?"

"Yes" was all I could get out, I was so excited. I was sure I would be able to identify all the snakes I saw from now on. I could go into a full study. As Mr. Cilliers neared Pretorius-kop, I reminded him about the snake book.

He made a stop at his house and we all walked in to drink something cool. It was so hot that we had finished the water bottle which always dangled on the front grill of the Land Rover so it would stay cool.

I was amazed to see the black game ranger, Piet, plonk into one of the sofas in the lounge. The white people didn't usually allow this, and I saw him receive his Oros orange juice in a glass with ice, just like mine. I could hardly swallow my cold drink, I was in such amazement. Black people were only allowed in the kitchen with an enamel mug. This mug would also not be washed with the white people's dishes and it had its own place to stand, under the kitchen sink, next to the cleaning materials.

I made a mental note to ask Letitia about this—maybe Piet was not black after all, although he looked very black to me.

The next few days, I studied the snake book, and just in case I forgot the more difficult ones, I copied each snake onto a piece of paper and coloured it as precisely as I could get it with my colouring pencils.

The next week, I handed Mr. Cilliers his snake book back and said he could ask me anything about the snakes. He did, and laughed as he could not catch me out. He laughed until the corners of his eyes wrinkled and only bits of blue peeped out; he wiped tears away with the back of his rough hand. He admired my snake drawings and ruffled my hair playfully.

Letitia and I had to go back to school. The short break was over. Mr. Cilliers would drive us in the mornings to the large Skukuza Camp, where there were other children of the Kruger National Park employees. We were only fifteen kids in the class and the teacher divided her time between the different age groups. She taught in both English and Afrikaans and switched effortlessly according to the language of the child she was dealing with. She was kind and distracted and allowed us to do whatever we wanted when we were finished with our schoolwork. I spent hours reading *Jock of the Bushveld*. Then I would sit and draw from all the animal books. I was fixated on the hippo, and in art one day, asked the teacher to help me get a "wet look" on the skin so it would look real. She did, and I knew she loved art. She gave me a little set of watercolours and paper so I could practise at home, too. These days were uncomplicated and I felt so relieved to be able to complete all my homework in class.

The drive to and from school was amazing. We would always take a detour in the Land Rover to the waterhole, and I would sit and sketch the hippo roughly on pieces of paper, to copy and correct it later. Letitia was full of praise for my work and begged me to give her one to stick on her bedroom wall.

I thought it was a good idea and started sticking my artwork all over my bedroom walls.

That same evening, Mrs. A tore them off in a fury, shouting that this was not our house and I could not just destroy the paint with sticky tape all over. She did not even glance at my pictures; she just crumbled them into bits, and with every pull off the wall, she would shout, "this-is-not," tear, "our-house-or-your-bloody-house," tear, "where-you-can-just-destroy-it-as-you-please," tear, tear, tear.

That night on the windowsill, I cried and placed my swollen legs onto the cold of the cement to cool the stinging. My head hurt where she had pulled me by my hair down the passage to the bathroom to pee. I had got such a fright. I had just got used to the peaceful life and now my heart was beating so very fast again.

I heard the lion. I knew it was a younger one; he had an unpractised, smooth sound—his roar was clear but gentle. I told him how sad I was. I cried and only stopped when I thought I heard Mrs. A's footsteps coming down the passage. I was so very scared of her; I had to stay out her way for the next couple of days or else she would kill me. The soul flies were strangely absent until I concentrated. They were black and grey and flew so strangely around my head. They made me angry and I swiped at them, but to no avail: they just stayed so black. I felt anger, bitter, bitter anger, inside me, until I had to jump out of the window onto the grass to vomit until I was empty inside. I had this new feeling—I was cross. So very, very angry. My chin dropped and I spoke some more to the young lion.

The lion crept up close to my window and told me to be brave. As I slept on the windowsill, he told me to at least show I was brave even though I was not. He licked my swollen legs and stayed with me until I woke with the first bits of light of a new day on my face.

I tried to hide my legs on the ride to school, but I knew Letitia had seen them. She frowned but said nothing to me. My eyes were swollen, too, and this morning I had not even tried to make my hair flip like Letitia's. I just brushed and brushed until the loose hair fell out where it had been pulled the night before; luckily I had so much hair it made no difference.

The next day, Mr. Cilliers did not pick me up for school, but instead Mrs. A packed my clothes in a suitcase and told me I would go to the boarding school in White River from now on. She did not have time to look after me in the day. The drive to the school was in silence—not that we ever spoke too much to each other, anyway. The town's streets were shaded by flowering trees and it looked like a little paradise. The school was small and both Afrikaans and English. Mrs. A decided it was better for me to get instruction in Afrikaans. I was petrified of the matron, but she smiled and touched my cheek and I knew she might be okay.

The children here seemed so relaxed and walked around in bare feet. Some still had their school uniform on after school was out, and some didn't. It did not look like they had too many rules here. A few girls ran towards me to say hello and show me around; I looked behind me, thinking they were talking kindly to someone else, because this was a welcome I had not expected. The matron spoke with Mrs. A in the entrance and I said a quick goodbye. All the kids went home on the weekends; I would be driving with the tour bus on Fridays to Pretoriuskop.

It was not hard to catch up at school and I never felt singled out like before. One thing was sure: I would never run or let them know I was a fast runner. That way, I could hide gently behind my indistinctiveness and keep very quiet. The popular girls lost interest in me, but that did not matter too much to me.

At this school, you could speak either English or Afrikaans, and even mixing the two was fine. My hunger was under control and I seemed to get enough food. Boxes of oranges and naartjies were standing in the dining room; you could take some to enjoy anytime, as long as you ate it outside. This was the only rule I could make out. A very large black woman who called herself Mamma had implemented it.

Well, I loved Mamma. I would sit next to her in the shade in
the afternoons, peeling the potatoes and plonking them into a
large enamel dish filled with water. She had big, fat hands
which would swiftly peel many in no time. She would be
talking in Swazi to her friend who was washing the windows
and I would listen to their tongue. Soft rolls; I could
distinguish when they became annoyed or excited. At first
she did not want me to help her, but then she relented
because I sat there anyhow, staring at them as they talked.

The sun would shimmer through the leaves and land on her
puffy cheeks, which glistened from all the Vaseline she
rubbed on her face. Little trickles of sweat would roll down
her temples and drop onto her heavy bosom. She hardly
spoke to me, but the comfort of her hips touching my legs
caused stillness in my heart, the little soul flies would dance
around my head and the quiet hum of the bees in their hives
not far off made my afternoons perfect.

I sat waiting for her under the trees, doing my homework,
and then we would peel or chop vegetables for dinner. She
called me "skinny legs" and when I lifted my skirt and
danced in front of her, showing off my long, thin legs, she
laughed until the tears rolled over her cheeks. She would
search for her hanky between her bosoms and wipe the
laughter from her eyes.

On Fridays, I would see the big zebra-striped bus arrive and
would grab my bags and jump in. Oom Callie was the driver;
he had a wild moustache, the corners of which curled up at
the ends, way past his face.

He told me to sit near the front after I started becoming sick
when we drove where the pine trees cast shadows and
sunlight. It was the alternating specks of sun and shade
which made me feel so sick. As we neared this spot, Oom
Callie would pass me his safari hat to place low over my
eyes so I would not see the stripes of light. His hat smelled
of sweat and tobacco smoke and was still warm from his
head. I usually fell asleep in this position and he would wake

me with a soft whistle in my ear. All the tourists would have left the bus already and I would feel happy as I stepped into Pretoriuskop, shouting my thanks to Oom Callie for the ride home and the use of his hat.

Once a man in a big Cadillac came to collect me from the boarding school, on his way to Pretoriuskop. He introduced himself as Uncle JR from America. I was so excited to sit in the driver's seat of his car, except his steering wheel was on the other side, so I pretended to drive us and he laughed with his belly bouncing up and down. He had the most delicious sweets in his car; they were big and either white or pink with massive almonds inside. I could eat as many as I wished, but I wanted him to like me, so I only took as many as would fit in my hand and no more. The white or pink melted into my hands from sweat and Uncle JR chuckled because he said I did not have to take them all at once, but one by one out of the bag. Uncle JR gave me a little blue Holy Bible and wrote a message inside for me; "O Lord, thou art my trust from my youth. To dear Judy, with love from your Uncle JR." I had my name in the top corner; Judy Alexander.

Once nobody came to fetch me, but the pastor of the local church came for me and had me wait with them there until Uncle JR could take me to Pretoriuskop. I was invited to have lunch with them. The pastor's wife had the most beautiful red hair I had ever seen. She smiled kindly at me and gave me a soft hug. She had me seated and I watched her feed her little baby boy, who had a soft hint of the same red hair, sitting in his high chair. He laughed his orange food right out of his mouth, to the delight of his parents. I felt and saw love and warmth I had never seen in my life.

Then she dished me up on my plate a lunch I would never forget for the rest of my life. I got the same orange on my plate the baby ate; she explained it was butternut. She drizzled it with butter and the steak was big and delicious. A few green beans completed this meal, apart from the whitest mashed potatoes. She asked me if I wanted more and I saw the abundance of food still left in her friendly, simmering pots on the stove, just as if she were awaiting more mouths to feed. Her husband laughed into her face and gave her a gentle hug and said she was ready at any time to feed the entire world. I did have a little more butternut with the butter and wanted to move in with them forever. That little baby boy was so very lucky.

Letitia and I would whistle to each other over the fence to indicate we were home, in order for her father to call Mrs. A at the reception to get permission to pick me up for a game drive or a visit over at her house.

As the sun set slowly in the shape of a great big ball over a distant kopje, I would screw my eyes and stare till I could see the duikers and klipspringers bouncing on the rocks. Then we would drive closer, slowly, and there they would be, just a whisper, stare back into my eyes and be gone on their swift little hooves.

I saw the duiker standing small but in the perfect silhouette against the sunset and I gasped with amazement. Mr. Cilliers stopped. I felt tears in my eyes for this perfect picture, for the loneliness of the little buck and the quiet of nature. You could touch the deepest blue of the heaven above you and then God would brush in the distance in all the reds of His pallet. I knew instinctively this would remain as my favourite picture in my head.

We drove on further. The two-way radio started crackling an urgent call from some game rangers not far off about a poaching. This was becoming a regular scenario every weekend I was home, but I had never seen this and was not sure I wanted to. This time it was serious, because it involved the endangered White Rhino. We drove to where the other rangers were gathered, speaking in angry voices. The black rangers were explaining that they knew who the culprits doing all this were. Letitia and I were warned to stay in the Land Rover, so we did. Letitia explained to me what poaching was all about.

"It's people who set the most awful snares for these poor animals, and when they have died the most terrible of deaths, or are near dead, their tusks and, in this case, the horns are cut out and the rest of the carcass is just left behind!"

I was in utter shock. "Why?" I whispered.

Letitia explained that these horns and tusks were sold for muti, ornaments or jewellery. I started crying and Letitia warned me to stop or else her dad would not let us come back tomorrow to look. I wiped my eyes with the back of my hand and sat bravely.

Letitia begged her father to take us with him the next day on the investigation. He reluctantly gave in and got permission from Mrs. A to pick me up at five a.m. the next day. I went straight to bed with the alarm clock right next to me. I knew where to push the off button and watched the little reflective numbers in the dark until I fell asleep. My last thought was to force myself to be as brave as Letitia—no, as brave as the White Rhino.

I was up with the first sound of the alarm and waited outside to be picked up. Letitia was excited and I was pale. What if we came across these bad poachers and they killed us on the spot? Piet looked very tense and his jaw was twitching.

We drove towards the place where the rhino had been found the day before. There it lay. We were allowed to walk closer and look before the investigation. I was shocked to see the way the snare had worn tightly through the thick skin of the rhino's leg.

Piet answered my questions in a whisper. "They struggle for a long, long time, which does not help them—it only makes it worse because the snare tightens even more. Then, whether they are dead or not, those horns are sawed out of their heads."

I walked to the rhino's head and uttered soft words of pity. Blood was lying thick in the sand, and I stared as I imagined this animal trapped so cruelly, dying slowly of thirst and pain. He was clawed back and could not move, but for the leg being cut deeper and deeper through the tightness of the wires.

"This is terrible," was all I could manage in a whisper. I bit my trembling lip as I climbed back into the Land Rover. I knew I had to pretend to be okay or else Mr. Cilliers would not bring me on these trips again. I bit into the inside of my lip until the salty blood filled my mouth. It was the cruellest thing I had ever seen, the defenceless animal caught like that. It was unfair and I was angry.

After being dropped off at our house, Letitia asked me if I wanted her to teach me to ride a bicycle, but I was now scared and felt sick to my stomach and wanted to be by myself for a while.

The house was quiet. I walked slowly down the corridor to my room; the walls were spinning and I was scared I was going to faint. In the bathroom, I held my head under the cold water tap and felt my heart beat against the basin. I closed my eyes and allowed the water to run over my face. *I will be brave* was all I could think. I dried my head and face and looked at my reflection in the mirror. I was white and the freckles on my nose looked exaggerated. My blue eyes stared red back to me.

I kept on saying the refrain in my head: "I will be brave, brave like the rhino."

The proud rhino could make the earth tremble as it stomped away, its large, intimidating body, head held up high. Dust would explode around each foot as it crushed its way through the earth. This was not a cuddly animal at all—no, this animal caused you to look upon it with reverence and respect. Yet, this was the animal man could destroy and mutilate, until it curled into a mass of pain and surrendered. Man could be so cruel.

When I fell asleep that night, it was with the cry of the hyena in my ears; they were always hungry and scavenged whatever they could find. Mrs. A liked to compare me to a hyena. I hated them and tucked my head under my pillow in order not to hear them, but they penetrated; they had an evil sound, the sound of death.

* * *

My head popped up and I realised I had fallen asleep in the sitting position. The old lady was still snoring on her bench/bed, and I decided to find an empty compartment to move to. I walked up and down the corridor, looking to find either an empty space or the conductor, to ask him if I might move. I came across a rowdy, drunken group of men and knew I had to pass by them; first I contemplated turning back, but then decided to push on. They whistled and laughed and called me all the pet names they could think up and found themselves very funny. I excused myself in an assertive voice and rubbed past two very fat men. The laughter echoed in my ears as I walked on with tightly squeezed eyes, nearly straight into the conductor. He saw what had happened and escorted me back. As I passed them this time, they moved to the side and I hissed, "Drunken bastards!"

We found a new, solitary compartment. I only had my brown suitcase, so the move was easy. I fell back into the hard, green leather seat and started biting my nails, slowly and meticulously, from side to side. I knew I was sabotaging my own interview with South African Airways by biting into the flesh, but I continued to do so anyway.

My thoughts were chasing after the time in the Kruger National Park. It felt so long ago. Was I even there? I should have stayed there; there were so many places I could have hidden. I could have lived with the animals. Animals are better than humans, because humans want to destroy your spirit and step on you, just for the sake of it, just for fun, just because.

CHAPTER NINE

Saying Goodbye to My Kruger National Park

I saw many animal poachings over the next few weeks. I helped look at the wire construction of the snares. The snares were lodged into the flesh of the animal and it was hard to see exactly where the wires were between the blood and rotting flesh. The poachers used different types of snares and this made it possible to differentiate where these poachers came from. Some were more sophisticated and some not. The local people had more expertise and their snares reflected it. Piet grumbled that the people from the borders, Mozambique to the east of the Kruger Park and Zimbabwe to the north, used anything and everything to kill the innocent animals. But we were lower down in the Park and it was mostly local people placing the snares. Many meetings were held, as well as discussions with the local police, to help catch the poachers. Letitia's dad became very busy with this.

Letitia decided to teach me how to ride a bicycle. The day started out with a big, smiley sun and blue sky of happiness as we walked off to the swimming pool for the big lesson. We decided the dirt roads would be too difficult to learn on and it would be better to try it on the paved area around the swimming pool. I was pedalling bravely and felt Letitia running behind, holding on and shouting instructions. I relaxed my grip the way she said and calmed myself down; I knew I had to push on and that I could do it. Be brave, I told myself over and over, and then I saw Letitia lying on her towel on the grass. I had thought she was still helping me and I pedalled straight into the pool. We were laughing and drying out in the afternoon sun. I could ride a bicycle. I could not stop this new accomplishment and feeling of freedom as I pedalled, hair blowing in the wind.

Letitia allowed me to ride home while she ran alongside me. Mrs. A was standing outside the front door with her hands on her hips. Not a good sign. I was late for lunch. I heard Mrs. A ask Letitia if she could keep the bicycle for the afternoon. Letitia skipped on home while Mrs. A told me that if I loved riding a bicycle so much, I would do it all afternoon, and she wanted me to ride up and down past the house until she told me to stop.

My legs were hurting. I cried and could not see where I was going, which caused me to fall and walk on home. Mrs. A shouted me back onto the bicycle and forced me to ride up and down the road. Only when people started looking at us because I was crying louder did Mrs. A pull me off the bicycle by my hair and into the house. My knee was bleeding and burning, but she did not even look at it as I showed her I had been punished enough.

Her anger knocked into my shoulder as I hit the passage wall. It stung my cheeks, it raged into my ribs as I lay peeing all over the floor, it clawed my arms, into the flesh. My hair lay in small bundles over the floor and I could not look at the hatred burning in her brown eyes, because my eyes could not see anymore and I knew I must turn into the rhino, I must be brave, I must survive. At least I had done something to provoke this; the rhino was innocent and got treated worse.

I lay crying. I could not lift my head. My legs were stinging from the hiding with a shoe, which had caused cuts, and burned due to the urine trickling over them. I was out of control now; I was dying. I was sure my soul flies would never return. I saw them scatter in flight. If only I could die quickly. I knew this was what the rhino had wished, lying in the dust. I remembered God for a fleeting moment and thought I saw Him turn His head away. But I did not die.

* * *

I could see a glimmer of lights in the dark distance of the morning as the train moved along at its own pace. I believed all children went through what I did. I knew my very first thoughts about myself were that I was bad and not doing well enough to escape wrath.

I tried to make out the farmhouses in the distance, but it was still too dark. The farmer must have been sipping his coffee before going out to his land. I was not scared of hard work, and this was what I would do when I reached Pretoria, but for now I did not want to think of the future; it was still as dark as this uncertain morning. You could see the lights and silhouettes, but not totally clearly; not enough to make out exactly what it was all about. It was my past I was saying farewell to; my childhood was over and now it was my plan in action. At eighteen it was not easy to think of myself as an adult, but I had become an adult long, long ago. That day my shoulders started slumping down because I seemed to be the tallest in the class and that made me stand out, my nightmare. Kameeldrift, the place I went to next, became a haze of stories, those I read, those I lived, and my daydreams expelling all homework, math. I cannot remember too much about that time. No person comes to mind; not one who made my life bearable. Nobody was kind or cruel. I had a lot to be thankful for.

The train moved on, beating along on its' own pace. Like life, you cannot stop it or let it linger for a minute when the landscape is worth looking at a little longer. You have no control over it; it moves, and if it stops, where you don't want to be, you have no choice—you have to stop, too. See it through; if it crashes, derails and plunges into hell, you plunge with, without a choice.

Life so far, had been a life without a choice.

CHAPTER TEN

Deserted in Kameeldrift

I did not die that day, but bits of me would over the next few months, bit by bit. She loaded me off in a godforsaken piece of earth, Kameeldrift, outside Pretoria, at the new boarding school I would attend.

She said very little to me over the last few weeks. I never returned to White River; I never said goodbye to shiny-faced Mamma. I never said goodbye to Letitia or her dad. I said goodbye to all the animals as we drove out of the Kruger National Park for the last time. I had no tears left; I just stared at the grasslands I had grown to love. I opened my window to smell it one last time, but she shouted it closed. I promised the animals my undying love. I sent out my heart to the hippo mother protecting her child with her life, her body, her everything.

I would resume school in Afrikaans. The dorm rooms reminded me of Middelburg and I felt a shiver run down my spine as I walked down the cold corridor to my assigned bed and table. I spoke to no one and no one had any interest in me, except this boy in class with millions of pimples over his face. He tried to talk to me a few times; I ignored him until he too gave up.

On Sunday nights, I developed a ritual: I would eat with my normal hunger and then go to the bathroom. I would stare into the mirror, trying to find my soul flies, begging them to return, and then I would drink water until I vomited and was sent to the sick bay. The nurse would just shake her head and give me a letter to stay in bed on the Monday.

I did not do my homework and had no interest in any sport; I became pale and felt pale. I would hide in the library at any given opportunity, and I started reading. My first book was *The Wonderful Adventures of Nils* by Selma Lagerlöf. Nils travelled over land and sea with a flock of wild geese. This book was the beginning of dreams again.

I would borrow this book every so often and the library teacher would just shrug her shoulders. I slept with it under my pillow. I had no vision of a family that held me in its lap as I wanted to fall asleep; it was the feathers in the pillow, representing the wild geese, and a flight into the far-off sky—freedom and the feeling of escape. I stopped praying, I stopped looking in the mirror, I stopped smiling, I stopped trying to speak to anybody.

The escape into my own world was peaceful and uncomplicated. I had hunger pains which drove me into the neat vegetable gardens to steal radishes or turnips. I would sit behind the tool room, eating and imagining being somewhere in the book I was reading. I found that I felt fewer and fewer emotions, until tears would just run out of my eyes without me having sad thoughts. I would fight these moments with all my might because I was trying to be the rhino, turn into the rhino, be brave and without fear; to be without sadness or loneliness, numb and invisible. Sundays I vomited at night until I lay on the cold bathroom floor and someone would find the nurse to help me.

It was on the sixth of September, 1966, when Mrs. A came for me because the school had no idea what to do with me but knew something was wrong—hence the sickness on Sunday nights.

She did not even look at me as I climbed into the car. The matron, making sure this weird kid would not return, packed my suitcase.

We stopped in front of some official building and I was told to wait in a room, which looked like a doctor's office. I had no idea where I was. A man with a white coat offered me his hand, telling me he was a doctor of the mind and would like to help me if my heart was not happy. I looked into his soft blue eyes and his kind smile.

Then his door was flung open and his nurse stood crying in the door: "Dokter Verwoerd is geskiet!" (Dr. Verwoerd, Prime Minister of South Africa, had been shot).

That was the end of the session to sort out my mind. Mrs. A made another appointment for me and drove off, crying into her handkerchief. I never did get to talk about my mind and its problems; Dr. Verwoerd's death caused my soul to die. His name would in future trigger resentment, deeper than for just political reasons.

The weeks and months following the session at the psychiatrist ran into each other day by day. I started attending an English school, in Sunnyside, Pretoria. We lived nearby in a block of flats called "Werk en Leef" ("Work and Live"). The corners of Mrs. A's mouth turned downward as she explained the ironic name of the flats where we lived.

Roy was home, too, and we started to get to know each other a bit. He allowed me to play some of his records after he showed me how to place them on the record player without scratching the black vinyl. I felt good, getting a lot of praise from him. He would not make me a sandwich or get me something to drink when he did it for himself, but he was never unkind and just left the peanut butter jar open and told me to put it all away when I was finished.

I would walk home from school and enjoyed these quiet times with myself.

Aunty Rose returned and the evenings were filled either with laughter between her and Mrs. A, or shouting bouts and fits of anger as they flew into each other, speaking so fast and loud I could hardly make out what they said. Mostly it was about money. Aunty Rose was a travelling saleslady and I did not see her too often, but when she was around, she was kind.

Aunty Rose came home one night with a truck and unloaded a big machine with a band dangling from it. You put this band around your backside and then it vibrated all the fat away. With a lot of laughter and happiness, this became an evening ritual for the two of them, starting with whiskeys, then a shake by the belt and then tall glasses of pink diet milkshakes.

I passed my standard at school and was left mostly to myself for the December holiday. I walked to the library nearly every day or went to play in the park by myself. I was never bored; on waking in the morning, I already had a plan for the day. Roy had to keep an eye on me, but he did not care too much what I did, as long as I returned to the flat before dark. In the evenings I would hold a concert for everybody who wanted to see, using the large lounge window curtains as the stage. I started dreaming of becoming an actress one day. I wanted to sing "Madame Butterfly"; the audience would clap until I could not bow anymore. Aunty Rose said that was exactly what I would do one day.

Then came the day. Mrs. A was packing my suitcase while Roy was shouting his anger towards the government. Aunty Rose was crying hard and holding on to me as if she would never get to see me ever again. Mrs. A's jaw was clicking and her frown was deep and puzzling.

She sat me down and told me that my pathetic parents had succeeded in destroying everything she had done for me. I was going to Bloemfontein. It was the spring of 1968, and I was eleven years old.

CHAPTER ELEVEN
A Life Behind Bars

The trip to Ons Kinderhuis (Our Children's Home) was like so many of the trips we had taken before: in silence, with my suitcase in the back. I did not understand why she was giving me to this place. I knew this was not like the times she had dropped me off at the many boarding schools I had attended. She tried to explain that my parents had to readopt my brothers and me. I had to go to the children's home first and they needed to prove themselves, to learn to be good parents. Then the government would decide if we could go to them. I was quietly wondering who had taught the hippo to be such an excellent parent. Mrs. A told me my brothers were also at the children's home and it would be good for us to get to know each other. This frightened me even more, because I did not remember them at all.

I begged and cried and promised Mrs. A that I would be good and that she should please not leave me there permanently—I loved her. I held on to her jersey while she tried to tear me away from her. I held and cried and begged.

"Mammie, asseblief, mammie, moenie my hier los nie!" ("Mummy, please don't leave me here!")

She took me back to the car and sat down, speaking to me. "Judy, I am so, so sorry, but you have to be a brave girl right now."

I just cried more and asked her when I would see her again; when would she fetch me?

"Judy, I can't see you again. You have to get to know your own mother, and it's for the best."

This just sent me into more crying and screaming. The matron came outside and opened my door and pulled me out. I stood there, holding my hands out to Mrs. A as she drove off. I was not brave at all—how was I going to never see her again? What had I done to make her so angry with me? Why was I being punished this way—how would I be able to go on?

The matron walked me through a side door. She locked it from the inside with an enormous set of dangling keys. We walked along the longest corridor I had ever seen; I looked at my reflection in the shining floor.

I was given a bed and a chair with a seat section that opened into a box for my toothbrush, hairbrush and Bible. I started packing my things into a communal cupboard. I only had a small cubby-hole in which to fit my stuff, but Matron grabbed my clothes and said no, I would not be using any of this; it would stay locked in my suitcase until holiday time, when I might have it back. I received a church dress like the rest of the kids—white, with a white hat—as well as a school uniform and two rotating "dra-rokke" (day dresses). I hid my little transistor radio Aunty Rose had given me as a goodbye gift among the underwear I was allowed to keep. I knew the radio would be taboo here in this institution and that I might need this lifeline.

Matron escorted me to the dining hall, where forty-plus girls ranging in age were sitting, clanging the last bits of soup out of their plates. That was the only sound. Matron introduced me: "Dis Judy van der Walt. Gaan sit en eet." ("This is Judy van der Walt. Go sit and eat.") My stomach turned at hearing the surname I had been forced to forget. It did not seem like it was me she was talking to or about, and I stood frozen, staring into some of the girls' hollow eyes.

Matron shouted my name and I tripped forward and sat down. I wasn't hungry and watched as they scraped this white margarine over the thin brown slices of bread; each one had a little block of margarine the size of a die. I was not hungry now, but I would starve here. I too would look like these girls, sniffing and wiping their noses on their sleeves.

I had never been as scared in my life and felt sure I would not make it here. It was cold in my chest. I cried so hard inwardly that my heart was going to explode. I stared and they stared at me. I had long, healthy blonde hair, big blue eyes, and a pretty navy blue dress with a sailor collar. I was wearing ruffled bobby socks and patent leather shoes, shining like the floors of this place. I did not belong here, I knew it. I was scared.

Everybody bowed their heads and matron said the evening prayer. They stood up in a choir, standing behind their chairs like soldiers, and sang a hymn. My head shot up and I stared at these creatures. Their voices were beautiful; they sang loudly and with passion. Where did they get that from? Their faces did not belong to their voices—there were so many links missing in these scenes. I felt so unsure and uncertain about what to make of it all.

We all walked out in rows to our rooms. Fifteen beds, all lined up along the long wall. Mine was not made up, so I knew where to go. I received one sheet, a blanket and pillow cover. I walked to a bigger girl and asked her where I could get another sheet.

She placed her index finger under my chin and, in a cold voice, she replied, "My darling, you only get one sheet and you make a choice, our new little princess, to put it over the mattress with all the pee stains or to have it over you under the blanket. This is not a hotel."

She turned on her heel, but not before I saw the disgust for me in her eyes. I would have to watch my step here. This place was beyond cruel; it was filled with something so tangibly and quietly wrong and evil it gave me physical shivers up and down my spine as I started to make my bed.

Lying in the darkness, I searched for my heartbeat. It was quiet; my soul flies were missing. I tried to see out of the small window, but the burglar bars ended my gaze. The mattress was hard and lumpy, the blanket scratched.

I prayed like never before: "Jesus, please help me, I am scared, I don't know what my brothers look like—I can't even remember what either of my parents look like. This place is strange. Mommy threw me away; I don't know why she didn't stop them from finding me and bringing me back to my pathetic parents. Amen."

I sniffed a tear away and the girl next to me whispered, "Shut up, you're not a baby!"

The morning bell rang for us to get up and I followed what the other girls were doing. I knew this was an Afrikaans place, so the Catholic praying on our knees first thing was not done here. Everybody rushed, in a hushed and tired way. Washing faces, standing in line for a free toilet, making the beds with very sharp, neat edges. Everybody had a rag under each foot. I did not have any, thankfully, because that was just weird. All the little pairs of cloths were lined up in the bathroom and I saw they were marked with names so they would not get mixed up. I ran after one girl and watched her every move and did what she did until she turned around and hissed at me to get away from her.

My school dress was too wide. I knew how bad I looked; I got a glimpse in the one long mirror in the bathroom. The mirror had some wide cracks and pieces missing, but I saw. To prevent my hair from being cut again, I plaited it stiffly and neatly on either side of my face, behind my ears.

I fell in line in front of the dining room door just in time. We walked in and stood behind our chairs. A long prayer from the matron ended and the chairs scraped the floor as all the children plunged into their breakfast of maize porridge and a cup of rooibos tea. I ate because I knew this day might hold little other food for me. The eating was in silence, broken only by two girls fighting about something. The matron yelled and the two girls ended up on the floor, pulling each other's hair. Chairs crashed and the matron and some bigger girls threw them out of the room.

We were inspected as we lined up at the door. In this same line, we walked all the way to the school, about two blocks down the street. We passed some small houses with sad gardens. The moment we were out of the door, the girls started talking to each other and their hollow eyes showed little flickers of life. We walked past the boys' section; I knew my brothers were in there somewhere.

The girl walking next to me introduced herself as Charmaine. "You have to watch yourself and stay away from those big girls in the front—they're nasty and could hurt you real bad. They call themselves 'Liefies' ['lovies'], but they're very far from love or anything like that. Stay far away from them and never approach them for anything."

I said I would be careful. Charmaine gave me a run-down of the system and what to expect. The "Liefie" group got away with everything and the matron allowed them the freedom to do whatever they wanted; Charmaine called them the matron's disciples.

* * *

The train rocked back and forth as I wiped the tears streaming down my face. I never saw Mrs. A again in all the years in the children's home.

So many people called it an orphanage, but that was not what it was; not even one child I knew was an orphan there. We all had parents. Maybe being a bad parent makes you a non-existent parent, and that makes their children orphans.

Allowing myself to think back to that day in Bloemfontein brought back a type of pain I had only felt once in my life. I lost a mother that day. I loved her. I even loved her arched eyebrow; I loved the little droplets of sweat on her top lip; I loved the sound of her gold bangles chiming against each other; I loved the little beauty spot under her eye; I loved her smell of Chanel No. 5; I loved the slight and soft "r"s as she spoke English; I loved the sound of stockings swishing as she walked; I loved the cow's lick of her auburn hair. I loved her.

CHAPTER TWELVE

Hunger

The first day went by in a haze. I kept feeling a loss: I would never see her again. This was now my life. Previously I had always had hope she would fetch me; now she would not come for me, never; now this was all I had. I thought this was what it felt like to be in jail. This felt like hell. No, this was hell.

At the school, the "dorps kinders" (town children) clearly looked different to the children's home kids. Their blue uniform dresses were a bit bluer, newer. The boys' shoes were shinier and their grey school socks had the school colours on the top edge. They did not receive sandwiches at break from the round bread tin. They would walk by it with their own homemade, wrapped delicacies. We would walk past the teacher who held out the tin and made sure we only took one sandwich per child. In this line we walked out of the classroom; then I realised why they rushed to get to the front and get their sandwich first, because the sandwiches were finished by the time I walked by. The teacher just clicked her tongue and said she would ask if one of the other classes had a leftover sandwich for me. She was still talking under her breath about the incorrect amounts when I just walked out and past her.

I stood alone against the wall in the sun. I was watching some boys playing marbles; they were aggressive and eager, shuffling around and causing a red dust cloud to puff up around them. It made it hard to see the shiny marbles. It was not strange for me to be alone at break, only now I had this heavy, heavy burden of walking to the children's home that afternoon after school and the weird fear I had about it all.

Somebody nudged me from the side and handed me a sandwich wrapped in wax paper. She said the teacher had told her to bring it to me. It was like gold. I took it and said thank you but the bearer of this amazing gift had already run off.

I opened the wrapping slowly and smelled Rosa in my treasure—little old, black Rosa. She would make a sandwich just like this. I bit into the fresh scent of yeast and love. I chewed and dreamt of the shiny Vaseline face that had once loved me so very much. This was a much better sandwich than those brown, dry, jam-touched sandwiches the other kids had received. I saw my soul flies return and hold me ever so gently; they were so hurt and careful, they did not come too close, but they did return that day. They weren't the happy colour I would have liked them to be, but they were there, and I whispered into the yeasty bread a big thank-you to God.

Walking home after school was a dreaded venture, just as I had thought; at least we could walk anywhere and not in lines. I looked for ants on the ground as I stepped on each paving block without touching the lines. Some smaller boys came running behind me and grabbed the ends of my plaits, laughing and running away very fast. I wondered what my brothers looked like and started searching among the boys for them; I knew they were blonde, but that was all.

We changed into our "dra-rokke" (day dresses). Mine was pale yellow from many washes. I had a cardigan and although it was summer, I was cold, so I put it on too.

The matron came in and handed me two identical cloths with my name sewn into them. "Here you go, now you can participate in walking clean into the house. Remember, if you are disobedient here, you will run up and down the passage a hundred times with those cloths under your feet."

I placed them on the floor and studied how the other girls walked. It was not simple; you had to keep your toes on the front of the cloth all the time while your heels went up and down. I slipped and fell. One girl giggled and I looked at her and smiled back.

Charmaine helped me up and, looking carefully over at the bigger girls, took me by the hand and out of the door. We walked to the end of the corridor and into a little lobby where the linen closets were. She looked over her shoulder and whispered to me that she would help me and I must do just what she did and I would be okay.

I told her how scared I was and she said she understood but I should be brave and follow her.

Charmaine became my lifeline for the next days, until she was taken to the sick bay with TB. I did not understand what that was, but I knew she was in hospital, so she was very sick. I had found her on the floor next to her bed, holding her head and crying, and then she went to hospital. We all received a scratch on our arms to check if we had the same illness. I was all right.

Charmaine taught me how to hold my head down in the study room and not make eye contact with the big girl walking up and down our aisles between the desks, monitoring and hitting us on the head with a ruler. She said I should do all my homework very well because they bullied the dumb kids, the snobby kids and the smelly ones. She taught me how to not look like a snob, because that was what they thought I was.

I was not allowed to lift my head, but since having my chin on my chest was my favourite position, it was easy. I had been continuously taught to look the world square in its eyes, but this was not tolerated here, so I slumped my shoulders and dropped my eyes and chin and did my homework and washed myself very well. Charmaine showed me where the library was at school, but children my age were not allowed to make use of it.

After Charmaine went to hospital, I had nobody to stand with at break, and so I walked over to the library and stood outside and just stared into the world of books.

The routine became a ritual for the weekday, and then it was weekend and I saw how on Fridays, the bigger girls took longer to get ready for school. They would tuck part of their dresses in under their belts in order to shorten the skirt and show more of their legs. They also stood at the bathroom mirrors longer, talking about the boys and what they were planning for the weekend.

Saturday was housecleaning, and I was allocated the bathroom with two other girls. There was a roster on the wall: I saw my name on the bathroom roster for months ahead. It did not make me happy, but I scrubbed. The toilets were the worst, and as I was the new one, I had to do them. I saw blood on the toilet seats and walls and thought somebody was dying. I was sure; all six toilets had bloodstains and it made my stomach turn. In my mind's eye I could imagine these girls were bleeding to death and it must be due to this place and the unhappy state you could get into here. I cleaned and flushed and vomited a bit, without the others in the bathroom seeing me.

There were no mops, so down on our knees we meticulously scrubbed all the floors, then rinsed them with clean water and then polished. Then I had to shine them with new, dry pieces of old blanket. I started polishing and shining, but was shouted to a standstill. We had to do it in rhythm and in sync with each other. The big girl stood in the doorway and shouted: "Op-af-op-af-links-regs" (up-down-up-down-left-right). She called this in a loud, clear voice, and if we were out of rhythm she walked closer and stood on our feet or legs with her big body. My knees ached and I had to do my best to keep rhythm, but lost it a few times and she crunched my foot bones into the floor. She was fat and heavy. I bit my lip not to make a sound.

We were allowed to get up after moving: three rows of blocks on the floor on our knees all the way out of the bathroom. We had to get up and run with our cloths under our feet this time, around and around the basins. I kept up until on purpose the big girl stepped on the back of my cloth as I passed her and I went flying; I tumbled and fell onto the girl in front of me. They all laughed; the big girl laughed so much her cheeks were flushed and the red pimples covering her skin looked like they were going to pop.

I got up and frowned and was so sad, angry and sick to my stomach. I had tried so hard. She lined us all up and made us run around again. I would hasten past her every time so she would not do it again.

Matron dismissed us and we went in for lunch. It was Boerewors (South African sausage) and maize porridge. The gravy created dams of cold in the white hollow of the porridge and I ate as eagerly as the people around me did. Then it was resting time and we had to lie on our beds for an hour. No reading, no talking, just lie down or sleep. I stared at the beds around me. Some of the girls were not there. It was the first Saturday of the month and that meant they could go out for the day to their parents. Others just received an afternoon visit between four and six p.m. with their family on the facility's grounds. I saw some smaller girls rocking themselves from side to side. Some were sucking on their thumbs. The bigger ones would lie and stare at the ceiling with cold eyes. I tried all the positions. It was hard to sleep in the middle of the day, but I realised how tired I was when the bell went for us to get up. We could play outside in the courtyard.

There were six houses like ours in a row. In the distance was one set of gates, tall and locked. On the other side, towards the boys' hostel, were a swimming pool and the sick bay and storerooms with all the other staff accommodation. It reminded me of what I thought a jail would look like. Every building was painted exactly the same: chocolate brown from the ground up one third, and then dirty beige to the top, ending with a red rusted roof. Later, on closer evaluation, I saw the walls were just dirty, maybe not even beige.

I went to sit on the cement bench outside and watched as the girls formed little groups and started playing with more passion than I had seen in them yet. The little clump of girls were playing with their dolls, feeding them, playing and then feeding them again and again.

I washed my hair and was drying it in the sun when I saw two boys walk over the bridge towards our hostel. They were holding hands. You could see they were brothers: both had golden hair, too short to blow in the wind, but you could just imagine how beautiful it would have been if it were a little longer and not in this brush cut they had. The taller one asked the girls playing hopscotch something and they pointed to me.

I stood up slowly. I stopped brushing my hair. I think I stopped breathing. I knew. I walked over to them and we held on to each other, Petrus squeezed between Francois and me. I held tightly onto his grey shirt collar and cried with all the pain in my heart spilling onto the little golden head, which was trying to look up and understand. Francois kept saying how sorry he was. My blue eyes were reflecting in his. It was only when we found a quiet spot under a tree that we started talking.

Petrus was covering our toes with sand and laughed when we tried to scoot him away. He took out his little Dinky toy from his equally grey shirt pocket and made little roads around our legs. Francois said it was his fault I had been stolen. I said it was mine. I should have fought more the day Mrs. Alexander drove off with me and I should have jumped out of the moving car.

Francois sounded like a very wise and tired old man, although he was only thirteen years old. He had been told by our parents to look after us both here in the children's home, and that was what he would do. I told him how much I hated this place and he said we should be brave, because it would not be long and then we would be back with our mother. He explained that both our mother and father lived in Bloemfontein in order to see more of us, and that we would most probably go to one of them the next year on a permanent basis. We had to be brave for now.

Only after Francois had given me some details on how he was treated in his hostel did I realise it was not going badly with me at all. Boys received whippings more often than us girls, and the boys were very physical with each other—there were many fights all the time. Petrus had just come from the baby house to Francois' hostel and he protected him. At this, Francois gestured in Petrus' direction and, looking at him playing in the sand, I realised this was the weak one. He had the softest skin and chubby cheeks for such a thin little bird, with brown eyes, unlike our sky-blue eyes. He was just a little baby and defenceless; thank heavens Francois was taking care of him.

Francois would not speak about my years of kidnap and he said I better not say a word about the time I had spent with Mrs. A, or even mention her name, to my mother. I knew then they actually blamed me for being taken and not fleeing or doing something to get back to them. I never mentioned Mrs. A ever again.

Francois wiped Petrus' nose with his hanky and said they had to walk back, visiting hours were over. I walked a little way with them. Francois said we would stick together and that I had to stay strong. We would find each other at breaks at school. He explained where we would meet each other. He would help me with anything I needed, he said.

I asked him where I could find storybooks and he said he would get them for me. On the hope of this promise, I

endured whatever came my way over the weekend. I felt
light in my heart because I would see my brothers, both
sitting across from me in the gallery of the church, on
Sunday. Petrus lifted his little hand quietly and waved at me.
I smiled and this warmth came into my heart and my soul
flies were scattered all over the church's majestic ceiling.
The organ made them dance and come into me with a sigh. I
did not understand the dominee (reverend) or anything he
said; I saw my brothers sitting, smiling at me, and I smiled at
them as if we were sharing a special secret.

*   *   *

The sun was coming up over the distant mountains. I knew it
was just a few more hours and I would start my new life.
When I thought of my brothers, I wanted to cry. It was
always like that. Petrus went to live with my mother. She did
manage to get him out of the children's home to live with
her, but I never wanted to trade with him. He had his own
hell to live. They were so hungry in Cape Town; she made
him search in the better hotels' garbage for something to eat.
How many times did he see the raw reality of alcohol abuse?
No, I was happy with my own hell.

I felt the weariness of not sleeping much. The sunrays on the
train window played rainbow tricks; cubes of coloured light
filled the compartment. I wondered about my future. Now I
would make my own choices. I would decide to live a life of
freedom. Some of my survival instincts could relax, maybe.

CHAPTER THIRTEEN

Days in the Children's Home

This was life in hell. There were bars in front of the windows. No laughter. These children were so weird, and this thought was strange: I had always been the weird one and now I saw so many with the same pain in their eyes as in mine.

The little ones who allowed themselves a giggle or laugh stifled it as soon as it escaped. We talked in whispers down the corridors; any explosion of sound would usually be a fight in full force. The moment when this happened, everybody ran to the scene. Strangely, we all stood and stared with our hearts beating at full pace. I found myself hoping they wouldn't stop and get into each other more; your own anger spilled into these two fighting, and you were just grateful it was not you on the floor. The entangled girls spat at each other and pulled hair, scratching and calling each other names. We stared and some of the older girls cheered them on until the fight became more intense and dangerously out of control. Blood would be evident on both, but only later, when the storm was over, would you recognise who was bleeding and from where. The worst was when they had to get stitches; their wounds and fights would be a visual reminder of the pain within our hearts for weeks.

Matron would get one or two of her disciples out of their eager stares and bring the sprawling bodies to a standstill. Often Matron would get a blow or two as she separated them, and that would shock and frighten me so much. But she always got them to stop, even though you saw her white crimpelene dress exposing her enormously fat thighs to all the onlookers. A few girls would snicker behind their hands, knowing they wouldn't get caught doing so in all the chaos.

Our routines were disrupted with only a few incidents. Walking in line to the swimming pool on Wednesdays for an hour's swim in the afternoon. Being weighed in the nurse's room, which was right next to the storerooms where we received an allocation of second-hand clothes, from school to church wear, when we had outgrown what we had. We also received a bar of soap and toothpaste on a regular basis.

Standing in a row in front of the storeroom, waiting for my handout of underwear, I could see into the children's home principal's office. He was a big man, with an unruly moustache. He was dressed in a khaki-coloured shirt and trousers.

He walked outside towards us with his pipe dangling from his lips.

All the girls in the row chorused in one voice, "Middag, Meneer Schoeman!" ("Good afternoon, Mr. Schoeman!")

The next moment, he was standing next to me and asked me my name.

"Judy," I answered.

"Do you have a surname?"

"Yes, sir."

"And what, if I may ask, is it?"

"Alex...no, van der Walt."

"Oh, you're the kidnapped child."

At this, all the children stared at me. They had not known. I could feel all the questions in their eyes as they stared at me.

"Yes, sir."

"Well, you're not kidnapped anymore. We'll be a safe haven for you from now on."

"Yes, sir," I answered and hoped and wondered. Nobody could steal me from this place with the heavy bars on the windows.

Headache tablets were given at six in the evenings after dinner, when we stood in a row at our own house's sick room. Actually, it was not a room, it was a store room, and I prayed I would never get sick, because there was no window and only a small bed and mattress with massive pee stains on it.

I asked another girl what the strange smell in that room was. She explained it was "voetevet", feet fat, which was a lotion we used in the winter for dry and cracked hands and feet. It was actually the type of creamy lotion used on the udders of cows in order to milk them. I was even more disgusted.

The meals were always the highlight of my day; it would bring back some or other memory of someone who had loved me once. The green beans boiled with potatoes and onions and then mashed with a hint of pepper were Rosa smiling into me. The sticky cold porridge in the morning reminded me of Joyful in the kitchen at the Kruger National Park. The oranges next to our lunch plates squirted familiar scents into my nose of Mamma in White River. The pumpkin was yellow, like the butternut of the caring mother feeding her baby, the reverend's wife in White River.

Everybody around the dining hall would have their heads down, trying to eat as fast as they possibly could. It was not that delicious at all, quite watered down and bland, but it filled us and we ate fast just in case someone took it away before we had finished every morsel on our plates. The day my memories became so vivid that a tear dropped into my green beans was when a "disciple" pushed my entire face into my plate. Green beans stuck to my face and made me cry more. At this, the matron entered the hall and asked what the commotion was about.

"Hierdie parraoog het in haar bord kos aan die slaap geraak!" the girl shouted ("This frog-eyed girl fell asleep in her food!"). Everybody started laughing and the matron sent me out to the bedroom, with a punishment. It was two in the afternoon and very hot, but she shoved my bed into the direct sun streaming through the window, grabbed blankets off all the other beds and commanded that I climb in under all the blankets and sleep if I was so tired, until she let me out.

I was so hot and sad and felt so embarrassed. The other girls were going to be mad at me because the room was untidy now, and their beds unmade. I cried and was thirsty but stayed curled up in one position all the time. I was scared the matron was still in the room and watching me wriggling around, which would provoke more anger.

I bit the inside of my lip until I felt the salty blood fill my mouth and cried some more. Through closed eyes, I could see my soul flies wander off and fly out of the window. They were small enough to escape through the bars. Then I started to pray to Jesus to help me. I opened my eyes and saw the outline of the cross of Jesus in the bars. I would go three blocks across and four blocks down and I could see the cross clearly. I smiled and fell asleep.

It was not a visiting Saturday; I knew that because all the beds were filled with girls forced to have their afternoon nap. Only the big girls were sitting, protesting, up straight, painting toenails or fingernails. One girl was whispering to the other about the picture book she was reading. These books were forbidden here; they were love stories in comic strip format, only there were photos of people depicting a story. The girls giggled and became starry-eyed at the sight of these pictures. The girl closest to the door had to keep watch in case Matron appeared, which hardly happened because you could hear her snoring in her flat, which only had half walls. She loved her sleep. The girl painting her toenails reprimanded the two whispering girls and told them not to be "horny". They ignored her and kept on giggling.

The next moment, the matron stood in the door with her hair flattened on one side from her sleep. She looked very angry as she commanded me to get up, put shoes on and follow her. My mother was there with a special permission slip to see me.

My heart stopped. I slipped my shoes on and followed her to the front door. Through the window, I saw Francois standing with a frown and Petrus, smiling, clutching my mother's hand. I walked into a whiff of cheap hairspray and snuff. She clasped her arms around me and then pushed me back to take a closer look. Then she pushed me aside and rushed towards the matron, shouting that she had forgotten to take the special permission slip.

Matron took it from her and looked at her with so much disgust in her eyes I winced, seeing the raw hatred. My mother was totally oblivious to the way the matron looked at her as she rushed back to us. She first grabbed Petrus' hand and then hastily let it go to catch a sneeze in the blackest and dirtiest handkerchief I had ever seen. Then she took my hand and led us to a bench under a tree.

She unclasped her white handbag, stained with pen and lipstick, and offered us each a mint. She threw one in her own mouth and spat as she spoke, hurriedly jumping from one subject to another. I did not know this woman. She did not look too happy to see me—not unhappy, but so busy with her snuffbox and trying to make Francois smile and holding onto Petrus so hard on her lap.

I just stared at her. I tried to find my resemblance in her face. I had made up some between Mrs. A and myself, but knew it was not possible. This woman was my mother. I should look like her, but I saw nothing which looked like me. Brown, thinning hair sprayed to a standstill. Her brown eyes were jumping fast from one place to the other. Arched brows pencilled in. Her mouth a bright pink line, sucking on her mint with vigour.

"Mamma is so bly jy's by ons uiteindelik, Judy!" ("Mommy's so glad you're finally with us, Judy!"), she said whilst scrambling in her once-white handbag. She found what she was looking for, another dirty hanky, and blew her nose noisily.

Suddenly I saw Francois looking at me and I knew I had the same look of disgust in my eyes the matron had when she looked at my mother. I had turned into one of "them"; I had betrayed our family. I had become one of the outsiders who shunned us, those who were disgusted by us. I could not face Francois, but wondered if he did not see it.

Petrus had the happiest little brown eyes, looking up at my mother's face with so much adoration and love it broke my heart. He would still learn there is no such thing as motherly love; no such thing as the perfect embrace against a mother's heart, hearing the whisper into your hair of her adoration and unconditional affection. But it did not seem to bother Petrus: he took the crumbs he could get. He held her snuff-stained hand when it was quiet for a moment on his lap, placed his head against her heart, smiled and looked so happy. At that moment, I felt a hundred years old. The wisdom dawned on me all in one afternoon.

They walked me back to my house first and then the boys walked off with my mother. She waved a quick goodbye back, with promises of a weekend with her. I couldn't imagine. I was glad I didn't have to see Petrus cry when Francois had to pull him out of my mother's arms. I did not have to live with the sick thought of that vision. Imagining it was bad enough. I had such a headache that evening and vomited until the matron made me swallow some white liquid and sent me off to bed.

In church, I saw Petrus' sad little brown eyes and tried to make him smile; I pulled faces and squinted my eyes. He started to laugh and Francois nudged him to sit quietly. There they sat, Francois with his frown and Petrus with his sad little smile. I asked God what He had done to us. I stared at the majestic ceiling of the church and knew God was big, big enough to do good things for us. My mother and father would marry again and we would go to live with them.

Mother would complain with a smile as we trod the red, shiny porch with dust, running into our home after school and straight into the kitchen to eat the most tender lamb and mashed potatoes. I wiped a tear and saw Francois standing, looking at me. The men had stood for prayer and he had too, only his eyes weren't closed like everybody else's. I was shocked at that defiance and lack of respect, but he kept his eyes open and winked at me. I smiled, thinking how brave he was.

On Monday at short break, I would have to ask him how he did it; by long break I had to know how to have the strength he had. But as Monday came, we sat on the shady side of the small wall and watched the children play marbles in front of us. Everything seemed okay to me again and Francois frowned a little more gently. He did tell me to give my mother a break; she had had a hard time trying to get me back, and her life under my father was hell. She was doing the best she could. I could not reply. I tried to picture how my mother looked for me over the years, not knowing where I was. Now I had to be grateful we were together.

On the days we were very hungry, Francois would run over the road to "Oom Janie se kaffee", Uncle Janie's café. It was not allowed, but Francois was fearless. He would buy half-loaves of white bread. We sat huddled together and ate as fast as we could, because the other children would beg and bribe until the bread was all gone. I didn't know where he got the money from and did not ask him, either; just gratefully ate lumps of that fresh, warm bread.

It was in that week that Francois pulled out his "gift" for me from under his shirt. A book to read! I was so excited and thanked him without asking where he had borrowed it from, but he said it was mine to keep. This was the first introduction to the series of "Saartjie" books. I adored this main character: she had a life in total contrast to mine, but reading through a few of these books, not in sequence, but always given with a big smile by Francois, I realised what normal life for a girl my age, eleven years old, should be like. I adored the fact that she, like me, would never step on the lines which separated the concrete stepping blocks on the sidewalk. I loved the fact that she had some spunk, which I lacked but tried so hard to emulate. Through her, I realised how defeated I lived; how sad and depressed I was most of the time. She opened my life to self-examination. I fell so short. I wanted to be like Saartjie. I wanted to be Saartjie. It was easy to pretend; I would walk by myself to and from school and imagine myself to be Saartjie. On my way from school, I dreamt of walking into a warm and comforting home. I sat in the dining room, eating with my head lifted a bit more, pretending I was eating what Saartjie ate. I got in the bath at five in the afternoon and pretended I was in "her" bathroom. I saw the white walls around me with rose wallpaper on them. I watched the fluorescent lights in the ceiling of the bedroom turn into soft chandeliers; the bedding became soft, with butterflies on it, and smelt of frangipani. My life turned into a storybook. I nearly smiled.

The day came when I met my father. It was long break at school and Petrus and I were waiting for Francois to join us in our spot. Then we saw him rushing towards us, waving his arms for us to go to him. We walked and he rushed, telling us our father was at the side school gate and wanted to see us.

My heart raced. Petrus increased his speed, smiling. There at the fence he stood, a tall, balding man. He had a suit on and a white, pressed shirt; his tie matched the colour of his suit and he had a business suitcase in his hand. He looked very respectable.

I walked over slowly after the boys had hugged him. He looked at me like someone buying a horse. "You've grown up!"

I could not get a word out. He had the bluest eyes I had ever seen. He took my hand, it was wet, I shivered. We walked over the street to the Greek's café, where he bought us each a delicious chocolate éclair, filled with cream and drizzled with melted chocolate. We stood in a row outside the café and ate hurriedly, as we always did. My father went back into the café and bought three small milks for us to wash down the indulgence. He took out his white hanky from his pocket, spat on it and started to wipe the chocolate smudges off our faces. Francois objected and wiped his own mouth with his sleeve.

After he had taken us back across the street, the bell went and he said a hurried goodbye to the boys. He told me to wait a bit. He looked at me and I stared back into his equally piercing blue eyes. He told me he was glad we were now together and I must never go off with strangers like that. I wanted to reply that we were not together, and I had been given, I did not go out of my own free will. But all I did was nod. He asked me if the cat had got my tongue and I laughed back because I thought that was expected. I was scared of this man. But his words reassured me, as he told me how much he had looked for me and cried for me and could not function because I was simply missing. He wiped the tears forming in his eyes as he said he loved me more because he had nearly lost me. He pulled me close to him and hugged me. The smell of Old Spice and tobacco went up my nostrils but I felt nothing back; I did not know this man.

I ran into my class late and everybody looked at me. I checked in the reflection of the window to see if I still had chocolate on my mouth and gave it an extra wipe and sat down as quickly as possible. When the class was dismissed at the end of the day, the teacher held me back for a moment. She told me I was not allowed to see my father at break and, even less so, to cross the street to the café. I promised I would not let it happen again.

I stepped onto the sidewalk blocks; I skipped over the cracks and portions between as quickly as I could, not looking up as I ran-walked towards the children's home. Would this place become a safe haven?

*   *   *

As I watched the sun moving higher into the sky, I listened to the rhythm of the train. What if I stayed on this train forever? What would await me in Pretoria and my new life? At that stage I did not dream too much; life was hard and real.

My first plan of action would be to get into South African Airways. I had to go for an interview in front of a panel of judges. Would they weigh me and find me too light for the grand jobs they were offering? I wanted to aim high. I wanted to make it big, become something and be something. What did Francois accomplish? He had gone to work for Iskor, the iron manufacturer. Then, off to the army. He bought a car, a wonderful one. He was so proud when he showed me. It was green and he had a wooden cross hanging from the rear-view mirror. His hair grew long and his blue eyes avoided mine. He was free three years before me, let out of jail—not because you were good, but because you were old enough.

Francois wanted to become an architect and could not afford the studies. I wanted to study, too, in Bloemfontein. I was so excited to see the university. We spent an entire day exploring all the possibilities, walking the campus, receiving nods from students with arms piled full of books. I was just amazed at the wonder of it all. I wanted to study Drama and Art. The excitement. The plan. Then came the rejection. The Dutch Reformed Church did not grant bursaries for that choice of studies; it was a field from the devil, all that drama, and then combining it with art...! This was a path I had to avoid and not pursue. It was teaching I was allowed to study, and not all the evil of drama. My heart was shattered that day. My dream of studies were now gone. I would never be called a student.

But I thought how I will show them, as clear as that sun shone in the bluest of skies: I would make that interview with South African Airways, I would work my way up, and when I was old enough to apply to become an air hostess, I would show them. I would speak about far-away countries as if these places were a natural part of my life-style and being and I will surpass them.

CHAPTER FOURTEEN
Months in the Children's Home

I became so inquisitive about the magazines the kids weren't allowed to read. So much commotion, so many fights and punishments were due to these black-and-white picture books of love. I knew I had to see what it was all about, and Francois helped me get them. I sat at school during break, between the shelter of Francois and Petrus, looking at these books. But after not too long, I became bored with these books. I thought of a plan to bring these books to the bigger girls in order to get into their favour. I asked Francois what really was evil about these books; he said he thought it was because they depicted people kissing and because it made you lazy about reading, because you could just look at the pictures to get the story.

That was when I started to write plays. Only, the plays I started writing were not your average story, but the love stories I read in the "forbidden" books. At first I added pictures I drew, but Francois said they were not as good as the story, so I left them out. I made up the most wonderful events in my plays. The names I chose were all beautiful, except the evil one: to her or him I would allocate a mean-sounding name.

These "plays" became my total obsession and also those of the other girls. They would trade and beg me for more stories. I became popular with my 'books'. Nobody could take them away, because they were not forbidden, but the stories also transported these girls into worlds far beyond the one in which we lived. I would explain in detail everything about the "outside" world. The mother and father sitting at the dinner table with the loving stares from one to the other; the flowered tablecloth and the touching of their hands as they passed the food bowls to each other. Glances of love and adoration between two people—or anything, for that matter—were what the girls found intriguing. It could be a cute picture of two bears hugging each other and they would have fought to have it.

The new world I escaped into was writing these plays. I even wrote them in direct speech. This kept me busy for hours and I was left alone, unless it was free time just before we had to bathe at night, and then I would sit outside. The girls would come to ask me to tell them stories and what was going to happen in the next episode. I dreamt up stories, accumulation through a vivid imagination. My witch stories became the most popular at night and over weekends, and the scarier they became, the more the girls revered me.

My homework was neglected. I did not care too much for math and my marks brought a frown to my teachers' brow. I just passed each subject, but my stories were growing. They became my life. I did not have much expectation of seeing my mother and father, and it did not bother me. Every day Petrus would ask when he would see them again and Francois and I just made up stories why they were not around. Then they would abruptly turn up when not expected—always, of course, when it was not visiting hours or on parent weekend and always with a special permission slip. We would always sit in some sort of hope, but not much, of perhaps seeing them on a normal visiting day, when everybody's family would visit, and then just as you got used to the fact that they were not coming around, they popped up.

My mother, this time with a man in a blue Volkswagen Beetle. Rassie was his name; Uncle Rassie we were to call him.

Francois was even more moody than normal. His entire attitude showed how much he hated seeing my mother with a man. I, however, did not care too much; I preferred the fact that she had stopped with the black snuff and was smoking cigarettes now. Uncle Rassie gave me this big hug as if he knew me and kissed me on the lips. He smelt of alcohol and I was sure he saw the disgust in my eyes. He had this big moustache and laughed easily.

It was a big deal the first time we went out with them. We were going to visit with them on a smallholding near Bloemfontein. It belonged to Uncle Rassie's mother. It was fun to drive out the gates of the "prison", and I realised I had not seen any of this city I lived in. Petrus was very excited and sat on my mother's lap. He was looking into my mother's face with such adoration.

First stop, to my relief, was to get something to eat. We walked into Oom Janie's café with such pride. They said we could order anything we wanted. I wanted those vinegar-scented "slap" chips I smelt every day across the street from the school. My mother ordered a piece of fried fish on top of the chips and I became very excited. It was just so much abundance. I received my own can of Coca Cola and a few Wilson toffees and Chappies bubble gum.

We sat with our treasures on our lap as we pulled up at a motel on the way. Oom Rassie and my mom got out and said we needed to be good, eat our food and wait in the car. We did not even look at each other as we spoke between the bites of heaven. Francois helped Petrus with his pie, but I was in my own fish and chips world. When we were finished, we all climbed out of the car to clean ourselves off, on Francois' insistence. Then we piled right back in to get to the sweet stuff and our drinks.

Time went by. We were listening to the radio Oom Rassie had left on for us. Two swaying men walked out of the motel and Francois made us roll up the windows and lock the doors. Petrus fell asleep in the foetal position on the front seat and Francois and I played "I spy with my little eye", until eventually the two appeared, laughing very loudly.

Francois looked accusingly at them and said our day's visit was nearly over and we had not even left the car. My mother replied, "Ag, Francois!"

We drove to a park instead of the smallholding. We were disappointed. We did not even have a ball or something to play with, we complained. Oom Rassie pulled his socks off and rolled them into a tight ball and told us to go play with that while he and my mother lay sleeping under a tree. Petrus played by their feet and Francois just sat, frowning. I was bored, too, and wished I had my stories with me to write more. Francois looked at me and asked me if I knew what alcoholics were. I said I think I did. He pointed to the two sleeping under the tree and said that was what those two were. That was the moment I gave a name to the smell of wine I always detected on my mother's breath.

Francois explained they drank until they were drunk, like now, they passed out, and that was an alcoholic. I looked at them as if it all made sense to me, but it did not. Why would one drink so much? I asked Francois why they did not stop when it did this to them. He told me they couldn't; they couldn't stop and would never stop. They would stay dysfunctional like that forever.

I became worried like Francois and asked why we couldn't go and live with our father, because it looked like our mother had blown that chance.

He looked so sad with tears in his blue-turquoise eyes. He waited long to answer while pulling the grass next to him out of the ground, bit by bit until he had his crying under control. Then he said in that weary voice of his, "Pappa is ook 'n dronklap, Judy" ("Daddy is also a drunk").

My heart stopped. I now understood why Mrs. A had called them my pathetic parents. I knew that as long as they drank so much alcohol, we would not be able to live with them. I wondered when they would stop. My mother had said she would take us out of the children's home the next year. I hoped she stopped, because we wouldn't go to her if she did not.

My hopes of us living as a family fell to the ground and shattered, like the first raindrops that afternoon. Big and heavy they fell, smudging the earth with water. The grass bent under the weight of the drops; the bare spots of ground had indentations as the rain fell hard onto it. The smell of wet dirt filled my nostrils and I cried. Francois rocked me against his chest, telling me to keep hope and faith. They might stop their drinking before next year.

Francois watched Oom Rassie anxiously as he manoeuvred his car through the traffic. He was in a very bad mood after he woke up and scolded Petrus and then my mother and then vomited a bit. My mother placed her cigarette the wrong way round in her mouth and Francois turned it around for her before she lit it.

They dropped us off without getting out of the car. Petrus knew better than to cry this time. Francois held his little hand tight as they walked to the boys' section. Matron was cross because my mother was supposed to come into the hostel and sign me in, not just drop me off. She was talking under her breath, but I understood that she hated some kids' parents and my mother was definitely at the top of her list. That would not make my life there any easier. She did ask me what the smallholding had been like, where we visited for the day. I answered that it was so nice and they even had chickens and we had eaten freshly laid eggs. I smiled as I told the lie and acted out my added happiness by skipping off to my room.

I fell asleep that night, smelling stale alcohol breath. I was pleased to see one star through the window with the bars, the bars with the cross in them, if you looked at them in the right way, counting four blocks of window down and three across. I felt the blanket rough over my body. This was the night I started to pray for my parents to stop drinking alcohol. The reason for my miserable life was this alcohol, the most hated thing in my life. I woke in the middle of the night and tried to find my star of hope through the window; it was no longer there.

The next outing was with my father; it was awkward to see that big, neat man holding a little permission slip in his hands. He had received special permission to take the three of us out for the day. I felt a bit proud as he stood there. He was tall, much taller than Matron, and she was a very big woman. He had a suit on with a beautifully elegant tie, his white shirt crisp and clean. His shoes shone as bright as the floors and his blue eyes smiled peacefully into Matron's scrutinizing ones. He had very little hair on the top of his head, but it was combed in a neat manner. In fact, you could pull him through a ring. He looked like a famous actor or a real businessman.

He took my hand and led me out to where the boys were waiting. Petrus was smiling happily and I was glad to see that. Francois looked sceptical as always, and I wished something could make him smile. The frown between his eyes was nearly always there.

My father walked us out of the gate and off to the bus stop. He held my hand tight in his; I did not know if it was his or mine that was sweating, and I did not like the feeling. I was glad when he let go to get his money out for the bus tickets and I wiped my hands off on my dress. We climbed into the bus and my dad stood talking to the driver while we found our seats. Francois looked angry and said my father was trying to let us ride for free; he never had money. I sat up straight and felt excited because of our trip into town.

My father came to sit next to me and ordered the boys to sit across the aisle on the seats next to us, but not before he had shouted some angry words at the bus driver. He would cough and, when the bus driver looked in the rear-view mirror, my father would say more horrible things to the man. Francois said, "Here we go again." My father told him to shut up. Francois frowned more. We climbed off the bus in midtown and I looked at all the beautiful shops.

My dad stepped off the bus, hopped two steps forward to the still-open bus door and shouted a few more hateful words at the bus driver. Only after the bus pulled away did he look down at us as if he had never said anything rude, and smiled ever so sweetly and asked us to choose what we wanted for breakfast. Francois said anything; Petrus said everything, he was hungry; and I just stood there, not knowing what to choose. We ate breakfast at the Wimpy, delicious eggs and all.

He sipped two coffees and smiled as we ate. We walked over to a toy and hobby store and he bought Francois a new pocket knife; this made him smile—a little, anyhow. He bought Petrus a new Dinky toy and I received a new set of hankies with my initial on them, a curly "J". Then he bought me a Barbie doll, with an extra set of clothes. I nearly died, I was so happy. Mrs. A had said Barbie dolls were too extravagant. That was exactly what I loved about them.

Then we walked into a pharmacy and I saw him buy Francois and me some deodorant and good, smelly soap. Outside the store, my dad gave me a pink brush for my hair which he pulled out of his pocket. I was amazed how he had so much for me; I was so excited about all my gifts.

My father bent down to me and told me to look into his eyes. "I love you very, very much, Judy, always remember that." He did not accept my nod; he made me promise verbally that I loved him too.

Francois had a set frown for the day as we went to my father's boarding-house room in the afternoon. He went to sit on the edge of his bed and poured himself a whiskey. He laughed as we three looked at him and said he had spoilt us and now it was his turn to spoil himself with a little whiskey. I could not wait to get playing with my doll, and Petrus and I settled in a little corner of his room. We were happy. Francois sat outside the door on the step, inspecting his knife. Later, he carved a little piece of wood.

My father called me to sit next to him on the bed—he told me to leave the doll behind and talk to him first. All I wanted to do was play with the doll. I sat looking at the doll lying on the floor as my dad spoke. He told me how he had searched for me and how much he loved me and had been so scared that he would never see me again and that God had planned for us to be together now.

I looked around the room. He had a little two-plate stove with two cups standing neatly next to two plates, which sat neatly next to some cutlery laid out in formation. A few boxes were placed neatly, from large to small, against one wall, with a piece of curtain draped over them to look like a table. The curtains were a faded green with pink roses; the same curtaining covered a little cupboard, which held cereal, coffee, tea, creamer and sugar. His room was spotless. He had some painting on his easel. He must have just started to paint it, because it looked far from done. The lady's face was totally the wrong colour; my dad taught me later it was an undercoat.

He lit his pipe and exhaled little rings of smoke for me to catch like bangles around my arms, much to my and his delight. Petrus joined in and he laughed, too. My father started falling asleep, still holding my hand, and I could not wriggle it loose. I just sat there, watching him wake every now and again and drink glass after glass of whiskey until he fell into a deep sleep. Now I could get up and I whispered to Francois that I was hungry. He showed me some money my dad had given him to buy us lunch and we walked in silence to the nearest café to buy a pie each.

Francois walked us to the children's home that afternoon, after he had covered my father with a blanket, checked that the little stove was off and the curtains were drawn. He left a note next to my father's Bible on the side table.

I explained to Matron that I had walked alone from the boys' hostel; my dad had to turn back quickly to catch the last bus to his accommodation. She just shrugged her shoulders and mumbled under her breath about irresponsible people.

I rushed to my room to hide my gifts. I brushed my hair with long strokes that night, a few smaller girls admiring my beautiful brush. One of them told me I had better hide it or it would get stolen. I slept with all my gifts under my pillow that night and for many nights to follow, not showing my doll to anybody. Just before I fell asleep at night, I would run my finger over the Barbie's long, plastic hair and sigh and feel so rich and blessed. In the night, when I woke up, I would place all my gifts under my mattress just in case somebody saw them on waking.

The mundane of my life and routine became a security. On the evening dinner bell I would walk straight into the line which would take me into the dining room and to my allocated place. I would stand and think under the evening prayer, making little lines, following the wood grain with my finger on the back of the chair. I would look at the food in front of me and feel it going down my throat. Lunch was our big meal; dinner might be "melkkos" (milk food), a warm and sweet meal and supposed to be hot, but it would have been standing and formed a thick skin on top. The two slices of bread were brown and paper thin, and these would be hungry nights. My days were filled with trying to get enough to eat; I was always hungry, just like the other girls. The hunger lay pure in their eyes.

When we sat down to eat, we tried to stretch our meal in different ways. Some would gobble it down in a minute and look at the others eating with definite precision: they would measure each little bite onto their spoons and chew on it as if it was a mouthful of rubber, not wanting it to become fine. They would swallow slowly and I would stare and wonder if they enjoyed the tasteless stuff, while I ate more reluctantly than ever in my life. I would see the big girls eating tablespoons of peanut butter in the evening and wondered where they got it. I started to trade a play for a tablespoon of peanut butter before bedtime. This made me write more and more stories instead of telling them, and that way I could get something to eat at night.

I was still on bathroom duty; I still had to do the toilets, too. I never complained, because it was useless, anyway. My Saturday mornings were filled with such sadness; I did not understand it myself. I looked out of the one window in the bathroom, past the burglar bars, off into the bustling street. Car, after car, riding by. I would imagine they were off to downtown and the beautiful stores. Off, to do Saturday shopping with the family. Children in the backseat, deciding where and what they would eat for breakfast. Maybe the girl would get a new frock and her brother a new shirt.

Daydreaming became a part of my life and when my eyes stung with irritating tears, I would shake my head and concentrate again on cleaning until it all shone. There was one major obstacle in my view to the outside world: the burglar bars. I would feel myself banging my head slowly over and over against the metal of it, the tears streaming now. I felt the pain so deep and real, with no chance of anything changing in the future. My stomach would tie into a knot and I knew I had to get out of this place. My mother or father had to take me out of here; these burglar bars were pinching my throat closed, making me suffocate. I had become the rhino in the snare, and the more I struggled against it, the tighter the feeling became.

I did not hear from my mother for a long time and wondered where she was and if she was okay. I hoped and prayed every day that she would stop drinking so that we could live together as a family. Francois had no hope—I could see it in his weary eyes, the eyes of an old man. I felt so sorry for him. My aim became to make him laugh at school break. He discovered I was ticklish and he would chase me around and I loved him so much when he smiled.

We started thinking about the school vacation and whom we would be going to. Francois said that he and Petrus would sometimes go to my mother, but mostly they went to strangers, apart from each other. I could not imagine Petrus being without Francois. I became anxious and worried that one of us should be with him. I thought we would go to my mother; Francois said I should not bargain on that.

As the vacation came closer, more and more kids were told, via little slips of paper, with whom they would be spending the summer holiday. I was nervous because these slips were handed out after lunch and I had not got one yet. In anger, Matron would shout at us when we were naughty that those who had not heard where they were going for the holiday might not be invited by anybody.

I wondered if my parents had asked for us yet. Francois also became worried, because he was sure it was a bad sign for us. Either our parents had not requested us, or they were drinking and had forgotten about it.

The next day, Francois called my dad from a phone booth, and a week later, we received our invitation slips. I could not wait to get to school and find out where my brothers were going. Francois was going to strangers on a farm near Bothaville and Petrus and I were going to my mother. Francois was glad I would be there for Petrus; I was sad not to be able to see him the entire holiday. I would not spend a pretend family holiday with all of us together. Francois said he did not mind going to strangers, because sometimes they would buy you nice things. I thought at least he would not have to worry about the drinking. Francois told me what to do when my mother drank, but I could not even imagine it being a problem.

The night before the school closed, it was like a mad house as all the kids received their suitcases and packing started in all excitement. The clothes Mrs. A had given me were still in my suitcase; that life felt like a million years ago. I touched the tartan skirts and the sailor collar on the blue and white dress. I tried some on. They were awkwardly short, but Matron thought they were perfect. Our suitcases were pushed in under our beds. I lay in my bed after lights out, felt for my suitcase, found it and rubbed my hand over it. I was so excited it took me a long time to fall asleep.

CHAPTER FIFTEEN

The Summer Holiday

Francois said goodbye to me the next day at school and I promised him I would look after Petrus. He looked relieved to not have to deal with all the drinking and told me so. I wondered what could happen and frowned a little myself.

My mother and Uncle Rassie pulled the blue Volkswagen Beetle up to the front door and Petrus sat happily on my mother's lap. My mother walked up to the matron and signed me out.

Matron looked straight into my mother's eyes and said, "Hey, think of me when you throw that drink back!"

I looked sternly at Matron as if to say *she has stopped, don't you see that?* My mother, on the other hand, said Matron should behave herself and watch her mouth in front of the kids. Matron just laughed and did not say goodbye to me.

I was glad to be in the car and driving out of those gates for an entire holiday. I tried to see Francois at the boys' hostel as we drove by, but Petrus told me his holiday family had already fetched him in a black Mercedes Benz. I asked him how he knew it was a Mercedes and he said because Francois had told him so and it looked like his Dinky toy. He pulled out a little toy car, and it was a Mercedes Benz. I smiled and knew Francois might smile a little more this holiday, too.

A fear crept into my heart and strangled it as we stopped at the motel. They climbed out, but this time they took Petrus and myself along into the lounge. Petrus took his little cars with him and I my Barbie doll and brush. We sat and played as they sat and drank. They became jolly and made friends with another man and woman. The four drank and Petrus got hungry. They ordered us a plate of sandwiches and we went to sit together on a couch and ate and smiled at each other all the time. I had to walk Petrus to the bathroom. Much later, he fell asleep on the carpet at my mother's feet.

I was getting worried because it was late and we still had to get to the smallholding which belonged to Uncle Rassie's mother. The two couples started arguing and I sat staring at the fight until the manager threw us all out of the motel. Petrus began to cry and I held him tight in the backseat with me. We pulled off with haste, tyres screeching, and I started to pray that God would help us.

My mother laughed a lot and Uncle Rassie had to stop the car to vomit. It was into a dark night and a long, straight road we drove. Then we left the tarred road and drove fast over a dirt road. I could hear the gravel smashing the bottom of the car. My mother's head was bopping up and down; she was sleeping through it all. Petrus was sleeping, too. Uncle Rassie looked like he was worn out and wiped his eyes all the time.

When we pulled up to an old house, I sighed with relief. Dogs came barking all the way to the car and woke my mother. She stumbled out of the car and into the house. Uncle Rassie forgot Petrus and me and turned back to fetch us. I woke Petrus because I could not carry him. An ancient-looking lady appeared on the porch with a flashlight in her hand and scolded us. We stood dead still, afraid of the dogs. The old lady called the dogs and took Petrus by the hand, saying I should get our suitcases.

It was hard to open the boot at the front. I felt the dogs at my legs. I shivered and bit my lip when the old lady appeared next to me and, with her thin little arm, pulled the boot open. I took one suitcase and she the other; she slammed the boot closed and walked me into the house.

Petrus and I shared a little room with a little window. He was already sleeping on his bed with the blanket pulled over him. I wanted to go to the toilet badly and asked the old lady where I could find the toilet; she put the torch in my hand and told me "outside". I shivered again and she saw it. She said there was a pot under the bed and I should use that. She took the torch and shut the door as she left the room. I pulled my pyjamas on and looked at the pot under the bed. It was made of enamel with chipped roses painted on it. I sat on it and peeped over the edge of the bed to see if Petrus was sleeping. My need disappeared and I got off. I got on it a few times and eventually my need became too big; I just had to pee. I crawled back under the covers and looked out of the little window—the sky was clear and there were a thousand stars. I prayed that Jesus would look after us. I saw a shooting star, I thought, I hoped.

It was the shouting in the middle of the night that woke me. At first I did not know where I was and then I went to peep out of the bedroom door and saw my mother in the kitchen; she was holding a long knife. Uncle Rassie threw a chair at her. I closed the door very fast and climbed back into my bed. I was shivering and had to bite my lip to stop. I listened carefully to hear my mother's voice; that way I knew she was okay.

It was raining the next day and I felt awkward as I took Petrus by the hand out of the bedroom. There was a black woman in the kitchen; we sat down to warm white porridge.

Rassie's mother came into the kitchen with a frown on her small, wrinkled face. Later I realised she never smiled. She told us to keep ourselves busy—she had a lot to do and I was to expect my mother to sleep all day, but just then my mother appeared in the door in her nightdress. She still smelt like alcohol when she gave us each a hug. She sat down with Petrus on her lap.

I walked outside and stood dead still when the dogs came close. I held my hands out to them; they started licking me. I felt happy to see the dogs liked me and walked with them out into the yard. The drizzle was light and did not bother me. I watched Rassie's mother in the chicken coop, feeding them and taking out the eggs. Her legs were bandy and her little back was round, but she stepped lightly over the puddles and her hands were swift. She walked up to me and asked me to take the basket of eggs into the kitchen for her. Her eyes were grey as the day and as sad as the rain.

I walked very carefully with the basket loaded with eggs. I looked through the mesh screen door into the kitchen as my mother poured alcohol into her teacup and I felt the blood run out of my face. I took the eggs inside and ignored her.

Petrus looked so happy, playing on the floor with his little Dinky toys. He just wanted my mother's love; I, on the other hand, just needed someone to get me out of the hellhole children's home for good. I hated the children's home so much and would have done anything to get out of there. I could have killed my mother at that moment as she sat there, sipping the alcohol out of that teacup. She looked wearily into my eyes and straight back to the teacup. She sat, speaking very slowly to me, not looking into my accusing eyes.

She told me that looking for me for all those years since I had been kidnapped had taken the last drop of blood out of her. She was tired and fed up and didn't know how to go on. Rassie was her only help in this world. I had to be grateful that I had been found and placed in one of the best institutions in the country.

I croaked the words out of my throat. "Mammie, when will you be able to take us out of the children's home for good?"

"Soon, Judy, soon" was all she answered and she walked out of the kitchen, tears running down her face.

I felt bad because I had made her cry. Maybe she was doing the best she could. Where would she take us, anyhow? I didn't know if I wanted to live on this plot, either. I felt desperate, lonely and worried.

I took Petrus to the front porch and made up a little game for us to play. He spoke so little and so softly; it was fun when I heard him laugh from his belly, so I kept on doing silly little things to hear his laugh. After lunch, it rained harder, and I lay on the bed with Petrus and read a story to him until we both fell asleep.

Petrus and I played the summer days away. We discovered an old rusted truck in the yard behind the house, and pretended we were going on road trips. Petrus sat on a box at the wheel, smiling, his brown eyes shining with pleasure. The trees and grass around the truck turned into the seaside and cities with exciting night-lights. We explored and played in an imagination which spilled over into our meals back at the house; the pretend world was an escape for both of us. At night we were woken by screaming and fighting, but in the morning when we went into the kitchen for breakfast, it was all quiet, and both Petrus and I looked around carefully to see if we could see the destruction of the night before. We moved our beds next to each other and held hands when we both became frightened as the sounds ended up right at our closed door. One night, Rassie stumbled into our room. We pretended to be asleep. He kissed us with a blaze of alcohol fumes filling our nostrils with fear and disgust. I started praying every night when we lay there, scared. Petrus cried so easily. I felt so sorry for him. I asked Jesus to make Petrus brave and for all the alcohol in the world to dry up, run out or just disappear. Petrus would ask me if Jesus was a magician and I said I hoped so.

I missed my soul flies so much. They had left me so long ago and I realised I didn't have the special feeling to see them. I was so far from those soul flies, I wondered if they had ever been a part of my life.

On a Friday morning my mother told me we were going for a drive. She was looking better that day; I heard her running a bath. I stood at the open bathroom door, watching her brush her hair, wishing I could hug her and make things better, but she had an ice wall around her. I wanted to fill her bath with rose bubbles so she could also experience the wonder, the feeling of indulgence. I had no rose bubbles for her; the steam filled the bathroom as she stood in her white nightgown. It had a tear along the corner of the armpit and I wondered if she knew. I realised my mother needed a mother at that moment—somebody who could take care of her so she could take care of herself. I experienced my first feeling for my mother, the feeling that would become my relationship with her, all I felt for her: pity.

We left, all packed into the Volkswagen Beetle, to visit some of Rassie's friends on another plot. Rassie's mother said goodbye at the back door, and as I walked past her she pressed a five-Rand note into my hand. She whispered that I should call if we had trouble. I was so excited about the money that I pretended not to see the worried look in her eyes.

The people we visited were kind, but I could see they were very poor. Their house looked broken, but the food they had set out looked very good and Petrus and I tucked into it. It was plates of chips covered in salt and vinegar; Russian sausages were lying between with big slits across their delicious exposed skins. They had all kinds of sweets and we saw litres of Coke standing out with mismatched glasses.

I helped Petrus and then I went to fetch my own plate and sat down next to him on the step of the veranda. We looked at each other and smiled with oily lips; we whispered soft exclamations of joy. The adults were sitting on canvas beach chairs under a motorcar's shaded parking. They were chattering like birds. You could feel the excitement; the alcohol looked to be in the same abundance as the food. We knew we might have to sleep somewhere because my mother was going to be up drinking with the other people all night.

Petrus and I found a sofa on the veranda and shared it with a big brown dog. He was friendly and it made Petrus laugh when it licked his face.

We were woken when there was a terrible fight—we heard glass breaking. Scared, we held onto each other, and the dog snuggled closer too.

The second time I woke up, I felt a hand on my head. I tried to focus but could not see who it was; the silhouette against the night sky looked like a man. The brown dog growled and I moved further into the sofa. I smelt alcohol and became frightened but did not want to wake Petrus. The hand went in the front of my t-shirt and I felt a pinch which made me cry out. This startled the dog and it barked. The person's hand left with an angry grumble. The next morning, I walked with Petrus' hand in mine through the night's destruction. I could not believe how many people were sleeping in all the different spots all over the house. There was vomit all over the bathroom and Petrus and I had to pee in the outhouse. I felt the five Rand in my pocket and did not know what to do. I could not see my mother anywhere. Petrus started crying. I made him sit with the brown dog until I found her.

She was sleeping; I tried to shake her awake. She hit my hand away and I knew she was going to be of no help. I took Petrus and we walked to the road. I could not remember if I had to go left or right out of the dirt road and asked an old black man on a bicycle, who lifted his hat in greeting; I knew he would be helpful. We walked side by side and then I piggybacked Petrus and then we sat to rest. I made up a game to entice Petrus to walk a little faster, and then the blue Beetle slammed on brakes in a cloud of dust next to us.

My mother stumbled out of the car and grabbed Petrus. She looked at me harshly; foam was in the corners of her mouth as she shouted that I was not going to steal her baby, that one child was enough to be stolen away from her. I did not recognise her; she did not seem to recognise me, either. Rassie accelerated and they drove off with Petrus. I stood in disbelief and fright. What would happen to Petrus? I would have to walk back to make sure he was all right. I had promised Francois.

I arrived at the house so thirsty, awaiting more shouting from my mother. She walked right by me; it looked like she did not remember what had happened. I was so thirsty I grabbed the first glass I saw in the kitchen; I rinsed it, poured water in and brought it thirstily to my mouth, only to spit it all into the sink. It tasted like alcohol. My stomach turned. I rinsed my mouth under the running water; I cried and drank from my hand.

I went to look for Petrus. I found him in the backyard, eating a tomato. He was glad to see me and showed me the wooden box with tomatoes next to him. I was hungry so I ate some, only to sit hunched forward later with the most excruciating tummy pain. Petrus went to call my mother. Rassie came to see what all the fuss was about. He gave me a stern look and I knew he remembered that I had stolen Petrus. He said I deserved the tummy ache because I had acted like a real bitch. I went to lie on the brown dog's sofa; Petrus joined me. I was sweating and, when the pain eased for a minute in between the cramps, I would lie and listen to the grownups laughing and shouting outside under the carport.

When I woke, it was dark outside and I needed the toilet. Petrus was asleep next to the brown dog. How could I have slept an entire day? What was the time, and where were all the people? I walked slowly, straining my eyes in the dark, towards the outhouse; I was so scared I was shivering, but the fear of stepping into vomit in the bathroom frightened me even more. I felt the brown dog next to me as I walked, and patted his head. I left the door of the outhouse open as I sat down to relieve myself, shaking all over. My tummy was not doing so well and the brown dog moved away a bit. Softly I called him back. I found the toilet paper by feeling all over the wall next to me; at first I wanted to cry. I shook my head and walked back with the brown dog. I could not see a thing, but allowed the dog to show the way. I was so hungry and knew Petrus had to be, too.

The brown dog growled as two figures moved in a nearby car, but I whispered to him and walked by fast. In the kitchen, I found the bread bin and felt inside it. I took what felt like a loaf and peeped into the fridge; there was nothing but beer, but I used the fridge light to see what was in my hand. It was indeed a half loaf of bread. I walked out to our sofa and shared some with the brown dog, but kept a piece for Petrus, who was still fast asleep.

I was so relieved as the blue Beetle sped off from this smallholding with us inside. Rassie had a fight with another man about the beer, or lack of beer, so he decided to take us home—not without swinging by the closest liquor store. My mother's head hung strangely to one side. I hoped she was just asleep. Her blouse was torn and she had a cut over her brow. I was too scared to ask. Petrus obviously felt something was going on because he stayed safely in the backseat with me.

Arriving at Rassie's mother's small holding, a calmness came over me. After Rassie had helped my mother off to their room, Petrus and I climbed carefully out of the car and were ushered off by Rassie's mother to take a bath. Petrus bathed first and went to the kitchen, where the black lady gave him food. I looked back and saw her stroking Petrus' soft white hair. It made me want to cry. I sat in the bath and cried; there was so much sadness in my heart, it ran down my chin and into my bathwater.

It was Christmas. My mother put a little plastic tree in the lounge. She hung little bells and silver tinsel all over it—I thought it was too much but said nothing because it made Petrus smile. The gifts under the tree were few, but I knew they were for us. I had adjusted to the new role I played, pretending that everything was all right.

My mother and Rassie did not drink any alcohol, but there was so much tension.

I saw outside how the skinny black man cut the head off the chicken for Christmas dinner. The smell of hot feathers made me sick. Everything seemed so brutal. We sat at the little kitchen table wearing our Christmas hats which came out of the crackers, all trying to look happy, but I think we fooled only Petrus. He had his hat clipped at the back with a clothes peg to make it smaller, but that in turn made it heavy and it kept slipping off, to his delight. I could not eat the chicken. I could not look into Petrus' eyes. My mother sat sullen, sipping cup after cup of tea. I had hope and tried to find it in her eyes, but she looked down a lot, and the next day Rassie drove my mother off to the hospital. The nerves hospital; she was having a nervous breakdown, they said.

I never saw Rassie in the days to follow. Petrus and I spent many hours playing make-believe stories out in the yard. We were fed at meal times and we had regular baths. Petrus looked happy to be with me and the black kitchen lady loved him, too.

My mother came back from the nerves hospital a day before we had to go back to the children's home. Rassie took Petrus and me to buy a few luxuries for our new year: some pens, pencils and nice smelly soaps for me; Petrus got a new school suitcase and he proudly packed his colouring pencils in a row. We each had a ruler, eraser, sharpener and a little notebook. We decorated the front page of our notebooks and wrote Francois a letter about our nice summer holiday.

Ever since my mother had come back from the nerves hospital, she had been so angry. I stayed out of her way. When they loaded me off first at the hostel, I did not even cry. I stepped into my new school year with a less hungry look in my eyes. I had a sense of accomplishment—I just did not know of what.

*   *   *

The sound of the train lulled me into sleep. The sun was shining on my face and it became hot. I woke and wondered what time it was, frightened that I might have missed my stop in Pretoria. I looked out and saw the familiar scenery outside; we were not there yet, but getting closer. This thought awoke me entirely and I sat up straight. I was so scared and excited. I was eventually going to be free.

CHAPTER SIXTEEN
Years in the Children's Home

There were some changes at the children's home. We had a new person at the head of the place, a Dutch Reformed Church reverend. This was strange. But this was a Dutch Reformed Church institution and I suppose that was why. He was tall and thin and had a severe look in his steel-blue eyes. His nose had a sharp bend; he approached us with a swift walk. Dominee van Rooyen was his name. The kids nicknamed him "Kieriekop", which meant the head of a walking stick. New buildings were built for the offices, near the girls' dormitories.

A lot of things were changing. Mrs. van Rooyen cleared out the old stock rooms, which were filled with dusty, torn, old clothes; she had an intimidating nod to her head. Her hair was tied in a bun low on her neck and she had the same sharp features as her husband. But it was when she spoke that my head popped up and I stared at her. She had the most beautiful voice. It was like a soft whisper, but still clear, so you could understand what she said. She never raised her voice and spoke sharply to those who did around her. I overheard her tell one matron she should not shout at the girls, because they were not cattle. I realised we might be in for some good changes.

In the hostel, however, things were like they were before. In study hall, the older kids would walk by and slam our heads onto the desk. This caused a commotion when my chin struck the desk one day and I bit my tongue right through. Blood was pouring out of my mouth and over the carefully rounded numbers in my math book. I cried and shouted, blood squirting everywhere. I ran to the bathroom because I thought I had lost some teeth, but with all the tears and blood, I could not see anything.

Matron accompanied me down the dirt road to the nurse. I was holding a bundle of toilet paper in front of my mouth. In the sick bay, the nurse laid me down and gave me an injection. I was hysterical; my shouting drew Mrs. van Rooyen out of her office in the storeroom next door. She wanted to know what had happened and, in shock, I heard Matron say I had slipped and fallen and must have bitten my tongue. I shook my head from side to side, denying the story.

The beautiful voice penetrated my dazed brain. "Judy, tell me what happened."

Matron shot me an evil look and said she thought I should not talk right then, with all the bleeding and all. It was after Matron left that I had a chance to tell Mrs. van Rooyen about the head-slamming-into-the-desk ritual the older kids had with the young ones and the outcasts. My tongue was not too bad, according to the nurse, but I spoke slowly and drowsily, my eyes wanting to close all the time.

"And you're not young, Judy, so are you an outcast?"

My eyes fluttered open. "Oh, yes, I am!" I replied with shock that she couldn't see that, that was what I was.

"Why are you an outcast, Judy?"

"Because I'm awkward, dumb and ugly and new and they also think I'm a snob, because I talk like one."

"I think you talk very nicely."

"Thank you." My eyes did not want to stay open.

"Do the big girls bully you?"

"What is bully?" I did not understand.

"When others hurt or ridicule you for no apparent reason."

"Oh, no, they have a reason."

Mrs. van Rooyen was disappearing in a haze. "So, you believe you deserve it?"

"I think I'm lucky when they leave me alone."

Mrs. van Rooyen walked slowly out of the door while I went off into the most beautiful sleep I had ever had.

My life did not change much after this event, except the bigger girls walked rings around me. Having them leave me alone gave me such pleasure. I still hated everything else about my jail sentence in the children's home.

Saturdays were the worst: cleaning the bathroom, staring out of the window, seeing all the passing cars with happy families in them. I looked through the burglar bars and cried a little. Neither my father, nor my mother had been seen for a time, and my brothers and I visited each other at family visit times. We sat under the tree and watched Petrus play with his toys. Francois looked sullen and I tried to lift his spirits. He told me the athletic season was starting and said he ran very fast. I excitedly told him I did as well, and then we started running against each other with Petrus setting us off: "On your marks, get set, go!" He would shout it out loud and laugh as we dashed off the line we drew in the sand.

After study time in the afternoons, the athletes would put their sneakers on and go off to the sport field at school. This became my joy and delight. I had no sneakers but ran faster than all the girls in my age group with my bare feet. I took part in all the field activities, too, and found that I also jumped the highest and furthest in my age group. I stood at one end of the athletic field and stared out over it all and felt how this entire field had started to belong to me. Here I was in control; here I was best. This feeling of superiority caused a rush within me and every time I hit the sand in the long jump, the child taking the measurements would whistle in admiration and move the measuring stick a little further. I started a little crowd of admirers, waiting for me to jump further every time. They planted a little stick where the inter-school record was and I flew right by that by a few inches. Exclamations of excitement rang out and more children gathered. The teacher took over the measuring and even he smiled brightly at me. The same happened at the high jump. I smiled walking home, holding my head a little higher; a feeling of superiority washed over me. *I am good, I am good, I am good. Today I am good.* A small fear crept into my heart, thinking that maybe tomorrow this lucky ability would go away. *For today I am good.*

The athletic season became my escape. The sports field lay on my right as I walked down the street in the afternoon to school. After a line of tall bushes, it was suddenly there in front of me. I would stand still for a moment, look at it and feel the sense of belonging rush over me. The track around the rugby field was just dirt, nothing spectacular, but it was red with white lanes painted on it, and that was where I would land my feet just for a split second, until I felt like I was in flight, until I reached the final line and ran through it with exhilaration. The excitement built up in my chest and then I walked onto the start line to run, jump or fly.

I owned that sport field; I felt in control and happy, until I looked up one day to see my father standing behind the fence, looking at me. A chill ran down my spine as he gestured that I should go over to him. This was interrupting my moment. As I kissed him over the fence, I could smell the alcohol on his breath. He was dressed immaculately, but I saw he had difficulty standing up straight. I became repulsed and looked over my shoulder to see if anyone could see it too. The embarrassment.

I spoke to him in a rushed way; I had to get back to practice. He asked me if I had any money. I was shocked, and I told him so: I never have any money. Francois was also out on the sport field, practising, and he told me to send Francois over to him. He called me back as I rushed away and said: "Kiss your daddy, Judy!"

I did and wanted to vomit. My energy was drained. The fun of the day had melted away. In an instant, I was just Judy again. Judy, the girl with the alcoholic parents. The children's home child, the nothing.

From that day on, I would look over to the fence where he had appeared and I always felt relief when the spot was empty. That was when I could jump higher and further. I would win the race.

Athletics Day came and I tied my new "takkies" (sports sneakers). I was so happy about these shoes. I tried to run in them but the teacher said I could only wear them to the field and then take them off, since I ran better with bare feet. My heart dropped when I saw my father. Then I saw Francois next to him and the secret thumbs-up he showed me to indicate that my father was all right, not too drunk—or maybe, just maybe, not at all.

I kissed my father hello and went to get ready for my race. I did so well and later, when the sun was hot and the day was at its climax, I saw my father again. He was shouting at a man. I was one of the kids who broke a school record in the hundred metres and my father wanted me in the newspaper. He pushed me into a circle of four boys who had also broken records and were getting ready for their photo to be taken. As I stood amongst them, my father told the newspaperman that he should take the photo now. I felt awkward and said "sorry" to the man taking the photo; he just nodded his head and asked me my name and surname.

My father hugged me. I smelt the alcohol. I walked off over my athletic field towards my next event with tears so glassy in my eyes I could hardly see where I was going.

*   *   *

I sat up straight and stared at the train seat across from me, I felt cold and shivered, even if I tried, I could not remember how it started. It was the train that bothered my privates. I was just a baby girl, I think. I did not want to wake up; it was such a good dream. I was tired and did not want this disturbance. I could hear his voice whispering and I tried to move away, but his hand was too heavy and big. That was a long time ago.

CHAPTER SEVENTEEN

A Violation of My Entire Being

A relationship started on Saturday visit times with my father and it felt like this was what I had missed all my life. He was fun to be around. I thought that now it was different, because my father had told me a thousand times how much he loved me. He told me jokes and made me trust him. I loved this man. He said he would kill for me. I became used to his cold, sweaty hands and held onto him without being repulsed by it anymore. He listened when I told him how bad the people were in the children's home. He understood and hated them just like I did. He became my confidant. We had funny nicknames for the people who made me mad. He called the dominee "Kieriekop" just like me, and we laughed like good friends sharing a joke. He painted like I wanted to and he told me I would; he would teach me. He gave me money, a rare commodity for me, and it helped with the hunger and for bribes. I gave some to Francois and Petrus.

When Francois and Petrus were with us, it was different: he was more of a father and scolded more and he was less than a friend. Francois gave me angry looks. I was a betrayer, because at first we had been a team against our father and mother, but now I had bonded with my father.

On Saturdays, my father would give Francois money so he and Petrus could go to the movies and my father and I would sit and talk and paint in his little room. He had a box of paints just for me. I started to trust him even though he was drinking whiskey all the time. He made some funny jokes the more he drank and later he would just fall asleep on his bed, snoring.

One afternoon, with Francois and Petrus off at the movies, I sat next to him on the bed, drawing a man. He asked me if it was him I was drawing and I laughed, "No."

I looked at him and jumped off the bed and shouted; his pants zipper was open and it was a shock, what I saw with my young girl-eyes.

Why did he do this? Why did he spoil it all with this, why did he make me sit back next to him on the bed? Why did he make me touch it? Why did I have to do it every visit with him? Why did he steal my only and last little respect for myself?

I pushed the blade into the flesh of my wrist and the blood poured out with such a gush over the bathroom floor. All the children were in the church. I complained of a headache and felt one too, so I was allowed to skip church. I stared at the window with the burglar bars. Tears streamed down my face. Blood ran over my legs and into a puddle over the floor. I cut the hand that had to do the shameful things. I had to use my left hand to cut with the blade the hand I wanted to remove from my body. I sat there thinking how I had started walking with my hand behind my back, trying to hide it; I was ashamed of my hand and I even tried to sit on it, to hide it, but when I thought of all it had done, sitting on it did not help. This had been going on for months and I knew it would not end. I started walking with my chin buried in my chest in fear someone would see the shame in my eyes.

The blood was such a relief; I hated my hand, my life, my father. I did not want to die; I only wanted to remove my hand, and then he wouldn't ask me to do it again. Couldn't do it without a hand!

The blood was everywhere. I stared at the red. I had not yet cut through the entire wrist; I had just started and would have to cut more. More blood. I could not live with this hand anymore. I needed no courage: it was easy to cut into my flesh, just thinking of that moment when he groaned and that ghastly stuff came pouring over this hand, my hand. I wanted to die at that moment.

My soul flies returned on that day, and I started thinking of them as my spirit. As my tears dripped, I stared at the other side of the room—*don't look, don't look!* The spirit flies came into that room and stayed close by and helped me get through things I should not have seen or done as a young girl. Things I should not have seen or experienced and was forced to do.

I scrubbed my hand. The hot water from the kettle scalded but I could not wash my hand clean. He always gave me money when I walked back to the children's home. I left without Francois and Petrus. I could not face them. I would walk so fast, angry and sad. I was confused and hated everything about my life. I had thought he cared for me, but he just wanted me to do this to him. He gave me some money; I would buy a snack for myself at the corner café. I hated my father.

The blood stopped and I floated off to a far-away place. It became so quiet in my chest; my breathing settled and I did not want to vomit anymore, just sleep.

It was the big lights above my head that woke me. My father told me about sex as he sat there, making me thrust my hand up and down. Three headlights went rushing into my brain. The doctor stared into my eyes and asked me if I was awake. I grabbed my right hand with my left and felt it was still there. It was heavily bandaged. I cried. Not gentle tears. I was jerking and screaming and fighting the hands trying to keep me still. I kicked so hard I knocked a glass off a nurse's tray. This evil hand was still with me. I screamed and cried and felt my heart beating against my chest. The injection forced me into calmness; my tongue became thick in my mouth and I saw and remembered what he wanted me to do with my hand and I cried. The veins in my neck were bulging; I could feel it. I vomited and cried some more. The screaming was still in my head but I could not get it through my throat, or out of my mouth. I felt that I was still screaming, but the cries stopped in my throat; I screamed again and again, but no sound came out. My eyes were heavy and the tears just ran out of them involuntarily.

The doctor and nurse shook their heads and said, "This one will try to commit suicide again!"

I felt like a prisoner. I saw the burglar bars and the cross was gone.

Nothing changed after all; only the scars were left on my wrist. I still had to do it in the years to follow with the same hand. Nothing changed. I changed.

*   *   *

God, why did I not refuse? Why had God not helped me? Why had God looked at this and not stopped it? I thought these things as the train continuously clicked its annoying click. Why had I been so stupid? It took me so many years to eventually get up the courage to tell my father one day, as he lay sideways in a drunken stupor, to fuck himself. I walked out. I had needed the money, I suppose.

That was all behind me now; it was nothing to me now and I was going to be free from today as I arrived in Pretoria. Unfortunately, I would have to live with my mother and Petrus for a year after leaving the children's home. I wondered why the welfare never scrutinised my hellish parents when I went to them for holidays. Now it felt like I was on probation from prison. What had I done wrong? What was my offence? Being a child, I guess. I was a child born to unfit parents.

I stared into nothing through the train window.

CHAPTER EIGHTEEN

The Strange Vacations of My Childhood

The children's home had its craziness: life was a hellhole most of the time, and small things like extra cheese in the morning for breakfast or an identifiable piece of meat for lunch made me happy. The seventh of March came; I thought it was my twelfth birthday. Mrs. Alexander had said it was. The children's home office told the matron I had it wrong: it was the eighth. I kicked up such a fuss on the seventh that Matron sent me to Ds. Van Rooyen to see my birth certificate.

I knocked on his office door and walked in. He sat looking tall and overpowering in his big black chair.

"Yes, Judy?"

"Dominee, for all my years I've celebrated my birthday on the seventh of March. Please let Matron know, because I missed my birthday now, the day is nearly over."

"Come look at your birth certificate, Judy—it is the eighth of March." He spoke patiently to me.

"No!"

"Look, your parents signed this when you were born, and you know that in your kidnapped years you didn't have this certificate to prove your correct birth date, so you got used to the wrong birthday date."

"No!"

He dismissed my frown. "Now that we have your birth date sorted out, we can move on. You'll have your birthday tomorrow."

I did not answer him but decided it was my birthday today. Mrs. A was more intelligent than my parents; she would have known.

"Another matter, Judy—I've scheduled you to see the psychologist on Wednesdays at four p.m."

"There's nothing wrong with me," I protested. On Wednesday netball practice started and I wanted to be part of it, but I said nothing about that.

"Oh, yes, you just don't know it. You've lived so long being dysfunctional that you don't even know how it is to be normal."

I winced at this. I was abnormal. I had always felt it. But I still did not need to talk to someone about it.

"I'm planning for you to have a good vacation this winter, with a good, well-established family here in Bloemfontein."

"My parents may want me to go to them!" I struggled, thinking that what my parents wanted to do and would end up doing was also an entirely different story. The children's home was open in the winter for kids who were not asked out, so I had better play my cards right. Even a strange family would be better than sitting here all winter.

"What about my brothers?" I asked.

Dominee cleared his throat; he was looking at the papers on his desk, but now he looked at me. "Well, I believe they'll be going to your father, since he has a full-time job now."

This was my cue to leave. Any questions about my father would get me into trouble, because he had made us promise to answer questions about his work, accommodation or anything else with definite answers he made us practise; I had never paid attention, or could not remember them all, because they were all made-up lies. He called it "twisting the truth" because the authorities were out to get him and he needed to be one step ahead of them.

I always wondered who this "them" was. I would see in my mind's eye the entire seating of deacons with their white ties in the church. Quiet, sullen-looking men working for a bigger force of unseen police somewhere. It was these dark, undercover men who reported to Dominee. My father said if I looked carefully in the home's offices, there were hidden microphones: everything got recorded and used against us in the end.

I excused myself and left the office. I looked at the ceiling for the microphones and realised they were very well hidden.

I had my birthday the next day and at small break, Francois bought bread and poured an entire packet of salt and vinegar chips in the hollow for us three to enjoy. At the second break, my father came, buying us éclairs at the corner café. My tummy was so full and I was happy. My father said he had a surprise for me and when he fetched us for the day on Saturday, he would give it to me.

I received a bicycle from my father on Saturday, a brand new green one, the name painted in gold, the most beautiful thing I had ever seen. Francois frowned, but my father said he would buy him something special for his birthday, too. I think Francois was jealous and in a bad mood when we walked back to the children's home. We had cake and sodas and it was a nice day.

I did not have to be alone with my father and that made me very happy.

I had to get special permission to keep the bicycle at the hostel. Matron was adamant that I had lost my mind if I thought she was going to allow it. My father told me to give it time; the authorities in the children's home were just not used to the fact that some parents bought their children the best gifts, the type of gifts the town children would get from their parents.

In the meantime, I rode on it when my father took us out for the day. I reluctantly stayed behind when Francois and

Petrus walked off to the movies; I stayed on the bicycle as long as I could, expecting my father to call me in, when my fun would be over and I would have to pay for this gift.

I pedalled fast, the tears creeping out of the corners of my eyes, the wind pulling the tears away over my face, streaking a line into my hair. Why could life not just be without pain? I flew past the houses and pedalled as fast as my legs would move me. A car swerved out for me and blew its horn, the driver shouting at me. I stopped and realised how far I had gone. I turned around and promised myself I would speed away from this hateful, disgusting life I had to live. One day I would have the courage to get away.

The winter vacation arrived and I went to people who owned a very big garage in downtown Bloemfontein. The day before, I said a hasty goodbye to my brothers. I had found a way to do it without feeling too much pain: ignore and step away, as if you were lifting yourself over it; avoid Petrus' big brown eyes and Francois' familiar frown. Don't look too deep and don't love too much.

A big, black car arrived for me. Mr. and Mrs. Havenga climbed out of the car. I wondered about this holiday. They were stiff and had stiff smiles. I got into the backseat, where a smaller girl was sitting, playing with her doll. They introduced me to Lollie. I smiled at her but she just looked at me.

The first thing the parents told me was that their daughter had kidney problems and I was to be a very good friend to her. She needed someone to play with her, quietly; because of her illness, she could not romp and run like other children and had to stay in bed some days. My heart dropped to my feet. No running the entire holiday would kill me, I was sure of that. I sighed and Mrs. Havenga gave me a stern look over her shoulder. Lollie glanced at me, too, and I knew I would be held hostage by this one.

We drove to the Natal coast the next day—Ramsgate. At the Shell garage, I saw how Mrs. Havenga would put Lollie's urine in a little glass and boil it to see how sick she was. If the urine turned white, she was ill; if it stayed clear, she was fine. I watched this little glass bottle with very eager eyes throughout the holiday: it predicted if we would move that day or not. These people took me on holiday with them to baby-sit their child. It had nothing to do with me; they did not care about me at all. The most they asked me was if my parents were divorced. Their main topic was their own child. I had to help her with everything.

I walked with her to the bathroom; I helped her with her hamburger; I tied her shoelaces, made her bed and brushed her hair. She was only one year younger than me, but could do hardly anything for herself. Her demeanour was that of a spoilt child and she expected all and more of the attention she was getting. I played what she wanted to play; every time, she would allocate me the inferior doll, the half-torn paper doll and the oldest Barbie with the bald head. It was no fun being with her. She often had to lie in her bed. When she fell asleep, I asked if I could walk outside; they usually said yes, and that was when I would run up and down the hill, as fast as I could. When I came home out of breath, no one would say anything to me as I sat down for dinner, exhilarated.

I knew Lollie hated me and I decided after a few days to treat her just the same as she would me. She complained to her mother that I was mean and did not want to play the games she wanted to. I received a scolding and was sent to bed without food for that evening. The kitchen maid tapped on my window and passed a bag to me; I looked into her brown face and kissed her hand holding the food. Black people were the only ones who loved me; at this stage, I knew that for a fact. I dreamt that night my first dream of many about my black mamma, always feeding me and tucking me warmly into bed. I would feel my own hand rubbing over the other, pretending or dreaming of the kind, soft, black hand stroking peace and love into me.

I woke early one morning and, in the toilet, found blood on the toilet paper. I wanted to cry. I had heard the big girls in the children's home talk of their period. I had no idea why, or how, but I knew it had something to do with babies and sex.

I was so frightened when I walked to the kitchen maid and told her softly that I had begun bleeding. She clasped her hands together, hugged me and clicked her tongue a thousand times, smiling, over and over. I smiled back through my tears, realising it must be something good. Mrs. Havenga walked into the kitchen and wanted to know what the commotion was all about.

The black woman exclaimed as if to share a fantastic secret, "Nonnatjie het groot meisie geword, Miesies!" ("The little girl has become a woman, Madam!")

Mrs. Havenga's eyebrows shot up and she grabbed my arm and pulled me with force to the sitting room. She closed the door hastily and grabbed both my shoulders and shook me fiercely. She told me that she had never wanted a girl my age with her little baby on holiday, but Dominee van Rooyen had convinced her I was a good girl. Now she sat with a major problem. I was not to tell anyone in the house about what had happened, least of all Lollie, as she was an innocent little girl and did not know anything about this type of stuff yet.

I started to tremble because now I knew there was something wrong with me. I was so confused and asked her how we could stop it.

"Stop what?" she asked in an angry whisper

"Stop the bleeding?"

"We can't, and that's the damn problem," she said, holding her head.

I became so anxious I started to cry again. She told me to wait and not move. I stood dead still. She came back with some money she placed in my hand, shutting my other hand over it and looking to see if someone had seen. Then she told me to go to the chemist down the end of the road and ask them for the stuff I would need for this dilemma.

I was so confused. I saw her leave the sitting room, looking over her shoulder at me once more, warning me to run off as fast as I could and not to tell a person what had happened to me.

I dressed fast and started down the road towards the chemist. It was a long way, but I enjoyed being by myself. The chemist was still closed when I got there. I waited in front of it.

A tall man in a white coat opened the door and asked what had brought me out so early.

"I have a problem," I said.

"Are you the orphan child the Havenga's brought with them on holiday?" he enquired.

"Yes, Doctor," I replied with a frown. "But I'm not an orphan."

"No?"

"No, my parents are both still alive."

"Oh, okay, that's what I meant—you're visiting with the Havenga's."

"Yes." Now he would know the secret I had to keep from everyone. I felt the tears trickle down my nose. I sniffed and he gave me tissue.

"What's wrong, my girl? And I'm not a doctor, but I might still be able to help you," he said and led me to a chair.

I told him I didn't think I could sit because I was bleeding down there.

This was a very clever man. He told me to wait a minute and came back with a pamphlet. It showed pictures of exactly what was happening to me. He gave me a pack of pads and asked me if I understood what was happening to my body. I said "no" and he sat in front of me on his haunches and described how the little eggs were not used, and it all turned into a soft fairytale.

He told me how Jesus had given me all these womanly parts that were not in use for making babies, but would one day be ready. I was not to have sex before I was married, because now I could have babies. He described what sex was. My mouth was dry and I stared at the man's grey curls at his temples; he had an easy smile and smiled throughout his story.

He took out a white pad from a packet, hooked its loops onto the belt and said that was how we would prevent the precious blood, or little, unused eggs, from staining my underwear. He smiled some more and touched my hand softly. "It's just like a big, soft Band Aid you'll need for a few days."

"So, this isn't an ugly secret?" I whispered through cracked lips.

"No, this is a good and big day in your life—who told you it was ugly?"

"Mrs. Havenga said I shouldn't tell anybody."

"Maybe only because she wants to tell her daughter herself about the wonder of menstruation."

"Oh," I muttered and added, "So I'm not going to die?"

"No, not at all, and quite the opposite—now you can make life."

"I don't want babies."

"You won't have them until you have sex, and you promised you'll have sex only when you're married."

"Yes," I said.

He sent me to the bathroom and stood outside the door, prompting me to do what the pamphlet showed I should. When I came out of the bathroom, he was still standing there, and he sent me back in to wash my hands thoroughly with warm water and soap. Then he handed me a parcel. I gave him the money Mrs. Havenga had given me, hoping it was enough.

The chemist smiled and said it was his gift to me and I could keep the money, as it was a very big day in my life and I was to think of it as special every month as it happened.

"Every month? I can hardly walk with this thing between my legs," I squeaked.

"Every month." He smiled. "Remember, it's something to celebrate. You'll get used to it. It's only for a few days—be brave."

As I walked back to the Havenga's' house, I thought of Madala; he had told me to be brave, too. It was so long since I had thought of the poor rhino and his brave fight for life. This thing bothering me as I walked would have to be; I would just have to be brave.

Back at the house, everything changed. I was given my meals in the kitchen and the three Havenga's went out alone, without me, but this changed my holiday immensely. I could sit with the black staff all day. I had my little parcel from the man at the chemist safely hidden with all its treasures: apart from the packs of pads, there was a bottle of perfume, roll-on deodorant in a floral bottle, the illustration pamphlet if I forgot what this menstruation thing was all about, and three candy bars.

The kitchen maid was the finest lady: she taught me to crochet and knit as we sat in the sun with our backs against the house wall. She would cover both our legs against the chilly wind with one of her beautiful crocheted blankets. On her day off, she would stay with me although I knew she missed her children, who lived with their grandmother in the township. She said she would catch up with them when the Havenga's were back in Bloemfontein.

I would run around and jump instead of walking and the kitchen maid would call out, "Little big girl has finished with the blood for the month and now she is jumping again!" and chuckle at her own joke. But it was true: I felt so free after those three days of changing one pad for the other and then, on strict instructions of Mrs. Havenga, burning them in a little fire outside until there were only ashes left.

Going back to the children's home was not too bad. I had my parcel from the chemist and my new crocheted blanket, a gift from the kitchen lady in Ramsgate, and a bag of shells another black lady had given me on our goodbye day. I told the other girls about the sea and how I had picked up all the shells in the bag and they stared at it with envy. Another wonderful vacation came to an end.

CHAPTER NINETEEN
The Endless Pit of Hell

The first session with the psychologist was uneventful. He was a young man and he had freckles over his entire face and reaching into his red hairline. He looked too young to be a person who knew how to deal with children. He asked about my vacation and I sat across from his desk, playing with my shoelaces. I said it was okay. I did not want to go into the details of this past vacation. I had already told the other children it was perfect, with long walks on the beach and picking up shells from the shore.

What if the Havenga family distorted my story or, even worse, told them I had not been into playing with Lollie? I started making knots in my shoelaces and wished myself out of the office.

He asked if anything fun had happened on vacation and I said yes, I had learnt to crochet and knit.

"And that made you happy? That you learnt to knit?"

"Yes, it did," I replied. Now I had six knots in my shoelace I needed to undo.

"The Havenga's were nice to you?"

My head bobbed up and I said a hasty "yes".

"Are you happy, Judy?" He frowned and searched my eyes.

I looked down and said I was okay. And that was the best a person could ask to feel—okay. I liked feeling okay. "Happy would be stretching it a bit."

"Why?"

"Because, Sir, I'm behind bars for as long as my parents drink alcohol and can't get me out of here, and I'd be lying if I said all that makes me happy!" I caught my breath and whispered a "sorry" and fell quiet.

This man was a total idiot; who the hell was going to be happy living in this hellhole?

"Right, then, this is all for today. I want to see you same place and time next week, Judy."

"I should be going to netball practice on these days, Sir."

"Well, that will have to wait until next season. You and I need to see each other quite a few times."

"Until I'm happy, Sir?"

"Until you're happy, yes."

"Well, that's easy, then—I'm happy now."

"No, you're far from happy. Remember what you did to yourself not so long ago." He looked at my wrist, the cut now just a scar.

I wanted to throw something at the man; he was so into his stupid job. Next week I was going to do an excellent job of being happy. All that made me happy was doing sport and I should tell this man so. If he wanted to know what made me unhappy, I would tell him: being taken away from sport, that made me unhappy.

The days in the children's home were more unbearable from one day to the next. But then suddenly one day our matron left and we were allocated a new matron, with a husband and two little children. They renovated the matron's section and they moved in. I felt shy when I met her. She had piercing brown eyes and short, pixie-style hair. She had a kind smile, but a stern look, too. Her husband was a police officer; the two children were so sweet and soft looking, especially when they were bathed and had their soft pyjamas on, carrying a whiff of baby powder, holding their teddies in their hands.

They wore bunny slippers and waddled down the corridors, smiling at everybody. The contrast made me clench my teeth when I looked at the smallest little girl in our dorm. She would have on her thinly patched pyjamas with all the print and colour washed right out of them, and under her feet would be the two grey cloths with her name on them to walk the floors to a shiny buff. This was the first time I had looked so closely at the little ones. Their eyes were hungry, hollow and avoiding mine. Neglected snot ran out of their noses. How could mothers sleep when they knew their babies were going through hell?

We were all still hungry. The food seemed so little, but I continued to see the hunger in the small ones' eyes and passed them some of mine. They would not thank me too much; they knew how to keep the attention away from themselves, and anyway, this was food—grab and eat while it was coming.

I watched these little girls with intensity and compared and it became a crazy thing in my head. They needed help; they needed care. I could not do it alone and realised they were like little animals, dodging or wincing when things got out of hand or when the big girls fought; they often wet themselves or their beds. They would eagerly run closer to touch a strange person, hoping maybe they would be hugged, loved, adopted or given a treat. They would call anybody who was around them for longer than a minute "Mommy".

I came to the shocking realization that it was pathetic, that all of us here in the children's home were pathetic. I was pathetic. I could do nothing about it; my parents could not look after me and that made me a pathetic case.

I started taking note of how people would look at us, at the church, the town children at the school: it was either with frowns of concern and pity, or even slight fear. I would prefer them to fear me than pity me. I gradually grew a hard edge around my mouth: instead of my lips turning upward in a happy smile, I would draw my lips into a thin line and keep it that way when I felt uncertain around strangers.

Another visit to the psychologist and I found a way to smile and tell him how much happier I felt. He would ask his trick questions and I would answer with perfectly rehearsed answers.

"How do you feel on weekends when your parents don't show up for visiting hours, Judy?"

"I've accepted the fact that they're busy. At least I have two wonderful brothers and we visit together."

"How are you doing at school? It seems you have trouble with many of the teachers?"

"I love school, but I have trouble with Math. The teacher said he would help me."

"Are you still so angry?"

"No, not at all, Sir."

"How do you deal with it when you get sad?"

"Oh, I pray, Sir."

"That's very good, Judy—I'm glad you've accepted the fact that your parents are never going to take you or your brothers out of the children's home."

"Yes, Sir." My eyes glazed. I swallowed and smiled my best smile, thinking of the sports field and its green, green grass in summer. I forced my mind to go far, far away.

"You have to make the best of your time here and grow into a strong person."

"Yes, Sir." I wanted to get the hell out of that office. I started pinching my arm; the pain was nothing in comparison to the hate I felt.

"You know you can come to me or Reverend van Rooyen with any problem or request."

"Yes, Sir, thank you, Sir, may I go now?" I could hardly breathe. I had to get out of this office.

"Yes, go."

"Thank you, Sir, good afternoon, Sir," I said cheerfully, biting the inside of my cheek.

I walked out of his office, past the old receptionist sitting hunched over her typewriter, into the sun outside and past children walking into the office. I stared into the blue sky and felt ice cold. My life would be here forever. I would never get out until I was finished with school. My heart was breaking. I could not face anybody. *I have been deserted, I have no parents, I will be here forever.*

I looked over at the burglar bars on the outside of the windows. I would never get out. I stood in the corner outside the house until my legs gave in under me, and I fell onto my knees and cried until I felt my insides burning. They were smothered cries because I did not want anybody to find me. I walked over to the tap in the garden and stuck my face under the cold water. I went inside, looking at the clock; I would run and make it to netball practice. I did not want to draw any attention to myself; quietly I signed myself out in the book in the corridor. I ran down the road and fell into my place in the warm-up exercises the other girls were already doing.

Then the game began and I played like my life depended on it. I received two warnings from the coach to stop elbowing the opponents, but I did not care—I was full of fury, hatred, anger and resentment. It was cold in my heart. I flew my elbow into the nose of the tall girl. Shouts and outrage against me; her nose was bleeding and I was sent off. I felt better. I did not care. I smiled and walked off.

I would get back at this unfair world. I would elbow and fight and do what I had to, because I was in this place forever. The world of hate had instantly become my world. This felt good. *Get them before they can get me*: that would become my motto. I knew for sure there was a God, just not around me; I was alone and would fight my fights for myself. I would become feared and never be fearful again.

CHAPTER TWENTY
Saturday Parents

We were such a lucky, blessed bunch of kids; Matron was echoing Ds. Van Rooyen's happy information. We had all been allocated a set of Saturday parents. Every second Saturday of the month, these "parents" would come and collect us and have us visit with them for the day.

My stomach turned when some of the kids asked if they could call these parents "Mommy and Daddy". At the information, they stood, staring, with glazed, happy faces. Were these kids crazy? They all had parents; how the hell could they betray their own so easily? I thought of it as another "pretend" day. These people were only doing this good deed to get into heaven, to look good, or out of their eternal pity.

Mr. and Mrs. Slabbert picked me up for my Saturday-parent day. I decided I would make them dislike me and give me up for another, more deserving and grateful child. I answered their questions politely. They had a daughter and son; the daughter was older than me and the son younger. I was slap-bang in the middle. The father was an architect, I found out when he showed me some of his building projects in his amazing study. The son practised his trumpet and then did homework and the daughter did homework and then practised the violin.

I could not have been more freaked out that day. The mother could cook very well and we all sat down for lunch. The dessert was sweet and soft and I felt hugged by somebody somewhere. Not by these people; they were not huggers. I thanked my lucky stars for that, at least. They had two bulldogs; I fell in love. Mozart and Baroque became my friends on those Saturdays. I would play with them on the lawn; I would roll down the slope and they would waddle after me, holding onto the ball. I laughed into their wrinkled coats; they slobbered me with their love. I always looked back out of the car window to see the last bit of them as I left.

The other Saturday parents would buy their "children" gifts, clothes and candy. The Slabbert family bought me nothing. I was sent home after the visit with nothing. Except on my birthday, they gave me a book, *The Prophet*. When I received this I had no idea, but this little book became my treasure. I understood very little but kept it hidden, and some days I would just stand and smell the pages. I wanted to read it but became confused, so I would just smell it.

The Slabbert family took me to my first ballet. It was a matinee at the city hall. I was stunned. I looked at these ballerinas barely touching the ground; in fact, they were drifting and flying over the stage, their tutus were as light as feathers and the music floated them back and forth. My mouth was hanging open. I had never seen anything so spectacular, so beautiful. I embarrassedly wiped the tears from my eyes. I knew with certainty that I had to become a ballerina.

Ballet became my obsession. I read as much I could about it. I stole a book out the library on Margot Fonteyn and Rudolf Nureyev and put it back a week later, just to take it again. One of the town girls in my class saw me reading the book and asked if I did ballet. She did; she became my best friend. She showed me some steps during break and I learnt eagerly. She laughed easily; her red ponytails bobbed up and down as she taught me. Susan became an enormous part of my day and life. She represented ballet and I loved her for sharing it with me.

One day she said she was going to see the movie with Margot and Rudolf, *Romeo and Juliet*. I nearly died. I begged her to take me with her. We schemed and planned and eventually her mother went to see Reverend Van Rooyen to ask his permission to take me for the weekend. I was overwhelmed and excited when they came to pick me up. Her mother was sweet and kind and, sitting in the movie, I had to pinch myself. I felt like my life was complete. Susan and I grabbed each other's hands during the movie when we became too excited to contain ourselves.

When we came home later that evening, her mother said we could play ballet and pulled a kist stuffed with ballet costumes out of the attic for us to play with. This was the first night that I never slept at all. We danced and dressed and floated over the creaking floorboards of Susan's room and into the passage and danced and danced and danced. It was the most magical night of my life, and my passion became an obsession with being able to dance ballet.

I planned to ask Reverend van Rooyen to let me take ballet lessons. I did not know how, but the seed had been planted and I started thinking about this all day, every day. I asked my father, but he said he did not have the money, and anyway, I should concentrate on athletics.

I walked with stiff legs and mumbling lips, rehearsing my speech, towards the office. The Reverend was kind and did not go crazy at my request. He did say he would have to find a sponsor for this and would let me know.

Two weeks later, I went off with the children's home van to the ballet shop to purchase my leotard and ballet shoes. Somebody had been kind and sponsored not only my ballet lessons but also my outfit to dance in. I was shaking as I put on one ballet slipper and then the other. I had to sew the laces and elastics on myself, but I knew I could do it.

Once a week, I would catch the bus and go to my ballet lessons. My hair was in a tight bun. The excitement and eagerness stayed with me until I sat, exhausted, on the bus back to the home. This became my life; I dreamt only ballet dreams and lived for compliments from Miss Borstlap as she nodded her head in approval. I had a lot of catching up to do and she reminded me of that all the time—I was the oldest and tallest in the class and was eager to jump ahead and dance with Susan in the same class.

My entire life changed. The other children in the Home envied me; I had special permission to leave hell once a week on the bus. I learnt to float and become graceful. I walked taller and held my head higher. Ballet became my escape from the real world.

Some of the older girls showed their jealousy by letting me do their chores. I spent more time cleaning after them and doing my own chores, but it was the only way. I had to stay humble around them or they would become hateful and turn against me. I was treading on thin ice and played their games all the time. I needed them to like me, or else my life would turn into a bigger hell. So, when they called, I ran; I cleaned their baths; they made me rub their feet and do their English homework. Their assigned Saturday cleaning I took over, which kept me busy for most of the day. I knew this was what I had to do to keep them from hating me too much.

The few free hours I would get I practised my ballet steps. I had to learn so much. The back veranda was mostly free and I would dance there every free minute. Nobody could see me there, and I kept the bathroom window ajar so I could hear when I was being called. I would stretch my legs on the windowsill and, because it was higher than the ballet bar, it was a good way to get my legs to go higher. In ballet, that was important: longer, higher, taller and thinner. I did my best at all of this, and the little food I was eating helped with the thinness, anyway. I started to tilt my chin upward; my shoulders rolled backwards, my neck grew inches longer because that was required of a prima ballerina. My ballet teacher would emphasize the same thing over and over: "Shoulders back, bottoms in, chin high, and grow long, beautiful necks. Look down your nose and elongate those

arms while the shoulders stay down but back and tall—
everything tall!"

I loved this woman with the soft, bobbing blonde curls. She
was short; I towered over her and she kept saying that length
and tall legs were good, very good. Everything I hated about
my body she loved. I did everything to make her give me a
nod of approval. The escape into the world of ballet totally
fitted my daydreaming, and while I did all my exercises, I
pretended to be a floating swan, combined with a white horse
galloping elegantly over the green hills. My life, my body
and my head changed. I would point my toes until they hurt.
While I polished the floors, I would point my toes, arch my
foot until it cramped; I would sleep on my tummy in order
for my toes to arch backward.

CHAPTER TWENTY-ONE

Another Dysfunctional Vacation

Petrus and Francois were both allocated vacation "parents". Two different families, but my brothers both seemed all right with the idea. I was to go to my mother. I dreaded the thought, but the last time she had come to visit, she had seemed a little better. Now that she smoked, she did not have those dreadful black snuff-stained fingernails. She even brought me some nice smelly soap and deodorant. She had hoped to get all three of us for the vacation, but it seemed I was better than none. I planned to practise my ballet and see if my mother would let me go watch some movies. I had some great plans; Francois had given me more books to read. It was the long Christmas holiday and the lazy days of summer lay ahead.

My mother fetched me on the bus. I had to carry my blue suitcase onto the bus and blushed when everybody looked at me. We said our goodbyes to Francois and Petrus and saw they both looked happy; I did not blame them. Their chances of disaster on their holiday were less than mine. But my mother said this time it would be different, and I believed her. She looked all fresh in her navy slacks and white top. Her white handbag was still full of stains, but I saw that at least she had some money in her purse.

She spoke to me in a whisper as the bus went along. "Judy, the Reverend wants me and you to develop a relationship. We were apart so long and we have to get to know each other again."

She went on about how hard she had looked for me and how that had made her very sad, and the only thing that made it a bit better was when she drank some wine. She thought she had lost me and needed that wine more often, and then she had four nervous breakdowns, which landed her in hospital. But now everything was fine and we would start a life together. Rassie and she had got married and were living in a town called Vanderbijlpark. Rassie worked at Yskor and was earning good money. They lived in a house.

I could not believe my ears and became so excited. This might be our chance. Our lives would change; they would be able to take us out of the children's home! My heart was beating so fast. I grabbed my mother's hand and told her how excited I was.

She looked at me for a long time without saying anything, and then she said she would have to try to get us out one by one, and she believed Petrus should be the first. I agreed, but felt good knowing there was hope for me to leave the hell I had to live in.

I told my mother I would wait. "They have started giving us two sheets now for our beds, and it feels so good not to have the scratchy blankets on my legs!"

"Judy, you must always be grateful and never complain. You of all people have so much to be thankful for. Where have you heard of any other little girl in your position being able to do ballet?"

I dropped my head and said I was grateful. My mother looked angry for the rest of the trip.

We switched buses and took the long-distance one from Bloemfontein to Vanderbijlpark. We bought sandwiches when we got onto the bus and sat next to each other in silence for most of the way. My mother broke the silence once to tell me that Petrus was the only one who suffered. He was just a baby and had had to be torn away from his mother. I sat there in disbelief, thinking it was hard for Francois and me too.

Then I said, "Francois is also sad and also has a hard time."

"Yes, Judy, I know you three children all suffer, but always remember that you and Francois are big and you two have your father. You two are different, you are fighters—not Petrus, he's a baby and a gentle spirit."

I understood what she meant about Petrus' spirit, but I did not think my mother knew how hard it was in the children's home. I told her so with a frown.

"Now, you listen to me—you are in the best institution in South Africa, better you cannot get. 'Ons Kinderhuis' is at the top of the list of homes and other children would give anything to be where you are. You are fed and clothed and you get a fantastic education. You have no gratitude, just like the Reverend said." She spat these words out in a whisper.

"Oh, he said that?" I hated that man, talking about me behind my back.

"Yes, and he said you act like a spoilt child. If you're not careful, that ballet sponsorship will be in jeopardy. You are the one of my three children who had a better life for so many years, and now you think life owes you something. Life owes you nothing, remember that."

"Oh, I've noticed that life owes and gives you nothing." I whispered these words in anger back in her face. I stared into her brown eyes, not dropping my lids for one moment.

I had seen this woman drunk, slumped in a stupor, and now she pretended to know it all. She had made me think it was my fault for being "stolen". I was kidnapped against my will and I would never forgive her for not finding me. Then, when I was found, she placed me in hell.

I looked down at my shirt and saw my heart beat against the cotton. I was so angry with the woman who was supposed to be my mother. She loved my brothers more than me; I was the intruder and now she was stuck with me the entire vacation.

"Eat your sandwich," she commanded.

I stood up and threw the entire sandwich out of the window.

She was so angry with me. She walked over to where I was still standing and said in a loud whisper in my ear, "You have done it again. You have done it just like your father did to me. I will buy myself a drink as soon as this bus stops and you will see!"

My head shot up and I felt a cold fear come over me. I felt the blood drain out of my face; I had to sit down before I fainted.

"Mommy, please don't, I beg you, I'm sorry, I'll never do that again, just please don't drink—I beg you, don't drink!" Tears were streaming down my face. She just looked at me.

Calmly she went to sit down. That became her weapon against me for as long as she lived.

The house was small and neat. I even had a room to myself. I began to feel better about the vacation. As soon as Rassie picked us up at the bus station, my mother told about him my escapade with the sandwich. He shot me a dirty look and I dropped my head; I knew then that I could cause her to drink with any acting out. I would be happy and behave and read my books.

The outward sign that everything was all right and my mother was not drinking was the red polished veranda: when it was shining, all was fine and I received some good meals.

On Fridays, Rassie would pick my mother and me up in his blue Volkswagen Beetle and sing the silliest song about blowing the pay cheque on payday. I realised that was exactly what they did, and it was famine or feast. Nothing in between. It was a roast leg of lamb and wonderful vegetables. My mother could cook very well and I experienced her love through her food. I was constantly hungry because I would dance ballet for hours every day. My mother said I was obsessed, but I did not care. This vacation was my time to catch up, so I could have ballet classes with my own age group.

Just before Christmas, things started going wrong. Rassie did not get up to go to work and my mother yelled at him; he had drunk too much the previous night and could not go to work. He had told me he drove cranes hundreds of metres above the ground. I felt it was better not to go to work because he could plunge to his death. My mother, however, carried on screaming at him at the top of her lungs. Eventually he got up to drink more and hit her. I locked my door and stayed there until they were both so drunk they passed out or it was quiet, for at least an hour.

Over the next few days, there was no shiny red veranda floor, no milk and a lot of fighting. The evidence was everywhere. I tried to put everything back to normal again. The holes in the doors I could do nothing about, but I tried to shine the red veranda. I only made a streaky mess.

The day Rassie stood with a pistol in his hand, I grabbed my drunken mother and ran. I heard a shot but did not look back. I knocked at the neighbour's house. The kindest woman took us in and we drew the curtains and peeped through to see what was happening at number five Darby Street. All was quiet. The kind neighbour gave my mother a lot of black coffee and me a plate of food.

This was the first of many police visits at number five Darby Street and I knew my mother had blown the chance to take us out of the children's home. I became so angry and resentful towards her, but the time Rassie hit me with a tomato box plank, I cracked. I spat at him and he went for me. I hid in the toilet as I heard my mother shout that I had better get out and run to the authorities. She shouted I should save myself, and I did. When the last of the toilet door gave in under Rassie's rage, I slipped through the smallest of the windows and jumped and ran. I ran away from one hell towards another.

I stood hitchhiking on the road that led in the direction of Bloemfontein. I had to get to my father. An older couple picked me up and gave me some of their coffee poured from a thermos flask, advising me how dangerous it was for me to be on the road so sparsely clad and that it was only God that led them to pick me up, not some evil person. The coffee was sweet and good and they did not ask too many questions. I lied anyway, saying that my mother had fallen ill and I was going to my father while she was in hospital.

The first thing my father did was take me to his neighbour and borrow a camera; my father looked so anxious when he realised he had no film, but then thought of his neighbour who might lend him his. He made me stand against the wall, ruffled my hair a little more and took photos. He took a lot of photos of my legs where the blue reflected the tomato box episode. Then he drove me to the police station to report the neglect of daughter by his divorced wife. I felt nauseated and saw hatred in my father's eyes towards my mother. But somehow he forgot about me. I was so scared and he did not make me feel safe. My father said that I would understand this, and thank him on the day when my mother would try to get us out of the children's home; he would show the authorities the photos of how I had looked on holiday to prove that she was an unfit parent. He now had physical proof of what a bad mother she was. I realised neither of my parents wanted the other to take us out of the home. They hated each other more selfishly than they desired to take us out of there.

I went to a place of safety for neglected and abused children. Juvenile delinquents had a section in this place. The woman behind the counter said I could not go back to the children's home because it was closed for the entire December vacation.

I walked into the greatest hell I had yet to experience. I had thought the children in the children's home were weird, but these kids were crazed and wild. The entire place had a disinfectant smell which stung my nose. Beds were lined up against one wall and there were no sheets or pillowcases. They handed me some clothes and a towel and sent me off to be scrubbed by a matron with no expression. I hesitated and protested, saying I could wash myself, but to no avail: here there was no privacy, no shower doors. I closed my eyes as this harsh woman washed me with impatience and hatred. I knew that moment where the disinfectant smell came from: the same substance that washed my hair and my body was used to wash the floors and anything else in need of deep cleaning.

That night, my desperate cries were poured into the dirty pillow. I had to stifle the noise and the ache was too big to worry about the stink in my face as I cried. In fact, it reminded me, between breaths, of why I was so sad.

I must have fallen asleep, because all of a sudden, I felt this warm hand looking for my privates under the blanket. I screamed so loud and raw I frightened myself. Lights went on and a matron and two large black women appeared in the entrance to our dormitory. The culprit flew under my bed, but too late—the matron and her helpers pulled a screaming, kicking, swearing animal out from under my bed. The girls started chanting "Butch bitch, butch bitch!"

I had not the faintest idea what was going on. I remembered the hand and realised it was the fat girl who was being pulled out of the room by her hair and arms.

My fear was now extended to fellow children, and I understood the haunting way everybody looked at each other. Your food was stolen if you sat down too slowly and could not hold onto your plate. We sat on long benches next to each other; two matrons and two black women would walk between us to see that nobody stole others' food. They each held a long stick in their hands and occasionally you would hear them use it on some unruly girl. All I could hear was the clanging of spoons on plates and sniffing children. It was jail. There were double-thick burglar bars on the windows, and all doors to the outside were locked. All the women in charge would walk around with the clinking of thousands of keys dangling from their waists.

My head became empty; I hoped my mother would not die under the hands of Rassie. I prayed to God to shorten the vacation and let me get back to the children's home as soon as possible.

I was standing at the window, looking out through more burglar bars keeping us inside, just dreaming of the day I would look out of windows without obstruction. The next moment a girl hit me so hard in the face I fell backwards. She screamed that I had gossiped about her. I did not know who she was, but I became enraged and jumped to my feet and slapped her back so hard she stumbled; we ended up on the floor and I scratched her face with every bit of anger inside me. My heart exploded as I bit into her arm. She screamed and more girls turned up; they pulled me to the toilets and pushed my head into the water and flushed the toilet—water was gushing over me and the floor and I found strength from inside and, rage oozing out of my veins, I could see the rhino fighting with all his power. I shoved backward at the three girls who were pushing me down and from my vocal cords a scream escaped which could have belonged to some animal. I became an animal, trapped by life, but decided at that moment I would fight; I would fight to survive and nobody would be my superior and I would rule the path of my life—with force, if needed, and I would kill if cornered.

I found myself sitting on the floor of a small room with a toilet, basin and a mattress on the floor. The adults had dragged me over here. I was in lockdown. My heart was still beating very fast and I was not finished fighting; in fact, I still wanted to kill.

A black woman brought me my food and placed it on the floor next to me as she said, "You nearly killed Tiger."

I asked in a raw voice, "Who's Tiger?"

"Tiger is the girl you fought. She said you gossiped about her and that was why she slapped you." Her brown eyes looked down at me. "You are a strong one—she is very beaten up."

"Me, strong?" I asked, my voice shaking.

"Yes, she had to get stitches because you slammed her head too hard against the bathroom wall. She is still in the doctor's room and will not get lockdown like you, even though she started the fight." With this, she squeaked on her rubber soles out of my cell and slammed the door shut. I heard all the locks shutting me in.

I had a week of solitary confinement, and when I came out, everybody looked fearfully in my direction. A new confidence overcame me and I played the role of "don't touch me or come too close—I can kill you". I loved this role. Everybody stayed well away from me; I was even enticed by bribes, but I ignored everybody. Tiger would not even look in my direction, but I saw what I had done to her: a bandage on her head, scratches, now with scabs on her face, a Band Aid on her arm. I looked and wondered how I had been capable of doing all that to another human.

My father came to visit me. He had not heard about my lockdown, or he did not mention it if he had. We sat in a small lounge and he pointed in the direction of the ceiling, saying nothing.

"What?" I asked back in a whisper.

My dad came close and whispered in my ear, "They have microphones and cameras and they are watching us."

"Who?" I asked.

"These people, Judy." He looked irritated because I was not catching on. He walked over to the matron at the front desk to ask permission to take a walk outside. She gave him a permission slip.

Once we were out of earshot, with good distance between the building and us, my father spoke again. He told me there were people listening to everything we said and could hold it against us when needed. I was confused but listened because he seemed so serious. They would hold anything against us, he said, and could even use it to prevent me from going back to the children's home.

My heart sank. I had ended up in the pits forever. My father said he would try to get me out for Christmas Day, and handed me a big slab of chocolate as he left. He hugged me too close to him. I did not care about going out on Christmas Day; if only I knew with certainty that I was going back to the children's home. I needed to have my ballet classes.

Every day in this institution called Tempe, I felt more and more isolated from everything. I became overwhelmingly sad and sat for most of the day in the sparse study area, reading. It became my escape. I did not practise my ballet; I did not want to be ridiculed, so I just practised my steps in my head.

Christmas Eve came and there was my father. He had permission to take me out for the day. On Christmas Day I could receive visitation on the premises, so off my father and I walked to the bus stop. I had to be back by eight p.m. This gave me an entire day away.

My father wanted me to hold his hand, but I told him I didn't like the sweat on his hands. He just shrugged. We had breakfast and then we were going to do some window-shopping. He said that having me with him over Christmas had caught him unawares and he had no job, so there would not be any presents, except for one thing, and that was a surprise.

My father was drinking a beer and I was sipping on a milkshake. It was hot, like every Christmas. Even so, the Father Christmas was all dressed up in his warm red outfit with layers of artificial beard and moustache. The reindeer were floating from the banisters and artificial snow and glitter was evident everywhere. Very, very festive. We were sitting in an atrium in town, watching all the people going

by. It was fun; I could let my imagination take over as I
imagined belonging to any of the families walking by. I
would choose one and then, on seeing a happier family, I
would change my mind and choose them. I would try to look
through their packets and parcels to see what was inside. A
fat man walked by; he looked like a farmer because of his
khaki clothes and dirty shoes. He had a smile and a silver
toaster box peeping out of his parcel. His wife was going to
be very excited tomorrow. Many of the people I saw were
going to be very happy tomorrow, and the day after, and all
the days after that.

Later in the evening, we had a hamburger dinner, and then
my father said he had something to show me. We went into a
building and took an elevator to the highest floor. We walked
up another flight of stairs and found ourselves on the roof of
the building. I walked slowly out onto the soft roof and
became scared. My father saw my hesitation and told me not
to worry. He walked closer to the edge and then sat down on
a pipe. His comfortable way around the place made me
realise he had been here before. He instructed me to sit down
next to him on the pipe. Then I looked out further: the view
was breathtaking. I could see forever. In the distance was
Naval Hill. The sun was setting. My father saw the
expression on my face and said he had known I would like
this surprise.

I stood up slowly and looked all around me. We were
definitely on the highest building in the area; you could see
the city all around. I felt so small and insignificant with the
vast space around me. My father touched my shoulder and I
shivered.

"Are you cold?"

"No."

"Are you sad?"

"A little."

"I want to tell you something." He cleared his throat. "Tonight I want to give you something."

I looked at him.

"I want you to look around you at the whole world out before you. Do you see all the lights down there?"

I hesitated. "Yes?"

"This, all of this." He waved his arm around the entire vastness before us.

"Yes?"

"This can all belong to you. You have a choice, Judy. Tonight I give you the world—tonight you'll know that you can have the world at your feet."

"How?" was all I said, thinking he has now lost his mind.

"By making the correct choices in life." He cleared his throat again and wiped the tears from his eyes. Then he continued, "You can have anything in the world—in fact, you can have the world, if you make an effort and just go for it."

I stood in disbelief; the thought that the entire world could belong to me was just too big.

I was just a girl and owning the world was impossible. I knew what my father meant; he meant I could do anything I wanted to. Still, that was a frightening thought, and I told him so. He said that fear could hold me back to the point where I attained nothing. He continued that I should become fearless, daring and spontaneous. Living in fear would hold me back.

Later, as we walked back to the bus stop, I made a strange connection in my head to a sermon I had heard one Sunday in church. The reverend had told the story of Satan telling God that he would give him everything he could see from up top there, if God jumped off the hill or mountain or something. He had to ask His angels to carry Him in order to prove He was God. I wondered if that was that what my father was doing to me—had he tempted me? He had not wanted me to jump off the building, but somehow this held a link; some weird connection was made in my mind.

Later that night in bed, lying on the bare mattress, I still remembered the view. I felt sure that my life would become fearless and I would have to force myself to dare more and never be intimidated. I looked around the room at all the children sleeping and felt myself superior; I felt myself grow and become great and saw myself doing great things. I fell asleep.

The day the children's home van came to pick me up at the place of safety, I felt such a big sense of relief. I was excited as I walked into the non-disinfectant smell; I touched the clean sheets on my bed and saw myself as privileged. I had more than many children, all the underprivileged children with their haunted eyes in the place of safety. The black-eye lined eyes of the teenage girls and their red lips always ready to snarl. They would display hostility against each other, and clearly also towards themselves. I was relieved to be where I was.

It was one day before anyone else came back and the matron took me into her little dining room to eat with her and her family. When we were eating the dinner she had cooked, she asked me what happened. I could not tell her the details of my ordeals. I could not tell her that my mother could not look after me and my father was not allowed to. How could I tell her that I had had the most terrible of holidays and that I was tired from all the nights in the place of safety, from the fear that some girl would come to my bed? I sat there and chewed on my rice too long and she let it go.

I watched the matron's little girls hopping on and off their chairs and eating bites in between their playing. They were dressed in their frilly summer pyjamas and smelt like flowers. It annoyed me to see such freedom and patience, which I had never experienced.

Later, in the bathroom, I stared at the blue circles under my eyes. I looked pale, the freckles clear on my nose; lack of sun and food was visible on my body. I looked thin and sick and I had never had time to practise my ballet. I was eager to get back into the routine of this place. At least I got to go out of the gates once a week to ballet.

When I tried my ballet slippers on, I found I had outgrown them. My skirt also felt awkwardly short. I went to tell Matron and she said she would speak to the Reverend. She added that there would be some changes in our future and we might have to forfeit a lot of things. Bloemfontein was experiencing a drought and we did not have enough food donations for this coming year. I stared at her; what did food have to do with my too-small ballet attire?

Ballet would once again be what I lived for. I would dance and catch up on the steps I had never practised; I would pour all my life into it again. I could close my eyes and hear the music, the soft rhythm of the piano music floating into my head. I loved it so much and could listen to it all the time. It was called classical music and I would sing it softly to myself as I floated across the dorm room. How I would love to live all by myself with nobody to stare at me as if I were strange. I could dance and make up dances; I would float and dance all day and night.

CHAPTER TWENTY-TWO

Days of Bewilderment

Francois and Petrus returned from their vacations changed, too. We even felt awkwardness as we stood together at break. Francois said Petrus and I should stand together at break times because he had stuff to do with his friends. I said it was okay, but as I watched his back walking away, I saw he was a little different, taller and a bit broader. There was a change in him. Even his hair seemed less blonde and his blue eyes avoided mine. He swore a few times and I looked at him in shock; we never cursed. He told me to get used to it, it was the way he was now.

Petrus decided he wanted to play with his new friends as well and I let him go, standing a few feet away, watching him. I suddenly felt alone again and thought about getting a friend for myself, but nobody would let me into their group. I walked over to the library and sat on the step, looking inside. I knew this was the year I would get my own library card. You could get a library card in high school, standard six; I was turning thirteen.

I had to wait for the fourth class on a Tuesday for that to happen. Then I would be allowed to take books out and sit inside and read. This would take up most of my time at breaks, when nobody let me into their game or made me feel bad.

The first book I took off the shelf of the library was the glorious, colourful adventure I had experienced before in Kameeldrift. I held the book gently in my hands. I felt the gloss of the cover under my fingers and put it up to my nose to smell it. It was the most amazing feeling: this book was larger than the normal ones. It was *The Adventures of Nils Holgersson*, written by Selma Lagerlöf.

I walked proudly to the teacher behind the desk who did the check-out. I had been watching children do this over and over from outside the door. I felt myself walking towards this check-out desk with my big, glossy book, and it evoked the feeling that I had a right to walk out of this library with a book lent to me.

The teacher told me as she stamped my library card that this was a brand new book and I was to look after it very well. I nodded and took the book from her hastily before she changed her mind.

Nils was a naughty boy with his own will and one very bad trait: he mistreated animals, which made me very mad at him. Then the dwarf turned Nils into a dwarf, too, and he left his house to fly off with a flock of wild geese to Lapland.

I cried and laughed through this book. The flock had a lot of adventures on their journey and Nils learnt many lessons about animals. I felt sorry for the geese when something bad happened to them and realised that Nils would make mistakes, but at least he tried; he was bold and acted fearless, although many times he was scared. I loved the different places the geese visited, and it awoke the first stirrings within me to travel and see the world. Bloemfontein was too small for me and I knew I would one day fly off, far away.

I nearly died as the teacher stood in front of the blackboard and I saw the large capital letters: "WRITE ABOUT YOURSELF". My mouth went dry as I stared into the blank pages on the desk in front of me; the ink stains of years ago engraved into the desk laughed at me as I tried to think of one thing to write. Usually I had so much to write about, but this was too much. I looked down at my legs and felt such resentment well up inside me that I was afraid I might vomit.

I stared at the page and back at the blackboard, hoping that the subject might change. Nothing would enter my head. I looked at my short-bitten nails and the sections where I had chewed into the skin and little crusts of scabs were developing. I started biting the scabs off. I wanted to run away. I wanted to change instantly so I would have something to say about myself. Nothing.

The teacher strolled through the paths separated by rows of desks. I felt his footsteps in my head as he approached and I tried to cover my blank pages with my arms. He stood dead still next to my desk and pushed my arms away from the pages with the long ruler he held in his hand. I could not look up. I always wrote my heart out in this class, but now, nothing. He spoke but my ears were singing and I did not hear his voice. He repeated his question, which made all the kids look in my direction. I fainted, slipping slowly down the chair, and my last sensation was the ache as my head hit the floor.

I opened my eyes, looking into a sea of faces trying to call out my name. I could see their mouths move but the sound was as if it was coming from a tin cylinder. I scrambled to my feet, pulling my dress over my exposed legs. My heart was beating again and I felt like a fool. The tears trickled over my cheeks; I tried to wipe them away. I was so ashamed.

The teacher escorted me to the nurse's office. She frowned at me, raised her eyebrows and asked in her deep cigarette voice, "Are you pregnant?"

I stared at her and whispered back, "Pregnant, how? Where? What?"

I thought she had lost her mind, but she insisted that I was old enough and could be pregnant. The teacher excused himself from the door. I could feel his resentment. I had seen so many older girls sent off to the house of unwed mothers. They were shunned as if they had some disease and my own disgust for them had grown out of what I had learnt from the other children. They had had sex. They had allowed a boy—

or, even worse, a man—to penetrate their privates for pleasure.

I thought I was going to vomit and squeaked the words so fast and so loud it did not even sound like my voice: "I am NOT pregnant, in fact I will NEVER be pregnant, and I am not ever going to be so pathetic!" I shouted at the nurse, finding I had walked right into her face and was staring into her bloodshot eyes. I remembered how the big girls in the reformatory were always scared of perhaps being pregnant.

"Okay, okay, I'm just asking."

I felt disgust for this woman standing in front of me. She dropped her eyes downward.

"I hate you people," I hissed at her. I felt myself grow taller and taller. I walked out of the sick bay and into the sun. I felt better and superior and thought I could write about myself. I would tell them, if they wanted to know, how wonderfully powerful I could be over people and that I was superior to most around me and that I would not step backward for anybody anymore.

I would never have a husband, let alone children. I would never put children on this earth, for the pain they would endure might be so much that even their own spirit flies forsook them. I wanted power and money, a lot of money to walk superior, even above and over the Havenga's of this world. I wanted to be famous and look down over my nose at the disgusting and pathetic of this world. I would be somebody and I knew God would help me.

I walked back into the class a changed person. I stared right back at the teacher and, as the sun lit my blank pages, I filled them with words. The Judy I created was stunning and strong and I knew I had changed forever. I knew I would rise above all the poverty, disgust and the pathetic fate that was dealt me, which I had inherited purely because I was my parents' child. I would and could make a change.

It was the end-of-the-day bell that brought me back. I handed my page in; it was not long, but it was powerful, and I knew I would become a new person on that day.

It was the day my life changed in so many ways.

CHAPTER TWENTY-THREE
Helena

There was a new kid in our dorm; everybody told the same story. She was with the matron and it had to do with her background, which was different from ours. Her father was in the parliament and her mother could not keep her any longer—she was a problem child. She intrigued me because I knew for certain she would not be like the other pathetic children; she would know and have more, be the type of person I wanted to surround myself with from now on. Distinguished people, better people, ones who would get me somewhere, or at the very least from whom I could learn. I had to climb out of my disgraceful past and the only way to do it at the moment was to be with a better class of person.

I tied my hair in two pigtails and put bright red ribbons over the elastic bands; they dangled as I move my head. I jumped into my field hockey outfit and grabbed my hockey stick and ran after Matron and the new kid, walking away towards the office.

"Mevrou, mevrou!" ("Missus, Missus") I called the matron, in order for her to stop so I could get a good look at this new kid. They stopped and looked at me. Helena's eyes changed from sad to inquisitive as she looked straight back into my eyes. She gave me a slight smile. I approved of her expensive clothes. I was happy to see it was not just a rumour.

I told Matron I was heading out for early practice hockey and she said it was okay, I just needed to sign out, and then she asked if I would like to show Helena around later and show her the ropes. I said I would be happy to and jogged off, knowing they were both still looking at me.

Helena became my life. She spoke English as well as I could and when we did not want the other kids to understand us, we would switch to it and enjoy their confused looks. I grew in this new superior role I was playing.

One Saturday morning, we were sitting outside, drying our freshly washed hair, when she looked over at me and asked me if I knew I had golden hair. I was confused. On her command, I had to hold up strands of hair in the sunlight and she told me to look at the golden lights in the strands; I looked and I saw it. She took a pair of scissors and snipped a new fringe just above my eyebrows. I looked into the mirror she held up with enjoyment in her face; I knew it had changed my face.

"Judy, you must know you're beautiful."

"Ag, you're crazy," I replied and kept looking in the mirror to see what she saw.

Helena put the mirror back in my hands and ordered me to look into it. "Look at your eyes, Judy."

"And what am I looking for?"

"Look at their colour."

"They're blue, Helena."

"Yes, what blue are they?"

"Blue."

"Some days your eyes are blue like the sky and some days your eyes are turquoise, and look, today they're baby blue."

"You're joking!" I replied with amazement, holding the mirror closer to look at my eyes. "You know I see little brown specks in the one eye."

"All I'm telling you is that you're beautiful and you have wondrous blue eyes." I stared back at her and said nothing, upon which she pulled my hair and laughed. "Say thank you, you idiot!"

"Thank you."

That night, while brushing my teeth, I looked at my eyes and my golden hair. I felt new and special and knew I had two beautiful assets I would have to get used to: golden hair and blue eyes.

On a Sunday, while we were supposed to be resting, Helena held a chocolate bar out to me. Our beds were next to each other. My life had changed.

I frowned and did not want to take her tuck shop sweets, but she insisted and watched me as I devoured it. She looked at me and said I was eating too fast. There was just a little piece left and she lay on her side and told me to stop eating. I stopped. I thought I had made a mistake; she might have just given me a bite, but she continued telling me how to eat it.

"Take little bites and let that lie on your tongue."

I did that and felt the brown liquid melt and trickle down my throat.

"Jislaaik," I said ("wow").

"You see, there's so much pleasure you're just hopping over—you haven't learnt to treasure or to savour."

"You'll teach me," I said.

"Yes, I will." She reached her hand out to mine and I took it. She gave it a squeeze and rolled over to take her afternoon nap.

Another Sunday, Helena decided it was time I had pierced ears. I was so scared but she coaxed me into bravery. I sat cross-legged on my bed and rubbed and rubbed my ear lobes until they were hot and felt dead. She made little dots with a pen, and the next moment, she took a needle she had been burning under a lighter and wiped it with mentholated spirits and I closed my eyes as I heard her say "no pain, no gain," and the needle went through and I had little rings of thread I had to pull back and forth and treat with the mentholated spirits so they would not get infected.

Every Sunday, another girl would get her ears pierced by Helena and I would sit proudly with my little string rings, encouraging them all.

My father nearly passed out when he saw my pierced ears, but I stood my ground and told him it was my life. All he could answer was, "You are turning into one of those kids," and I proudly told him that he had forced me to live there and that was why I was what I was. At that he poured his golden-brown liquor into his glass and took a big gulp, wiping his mouth with the back of his hand. He cried because I had hurt him and said I needed to come and sit next to him on the bed. I started trembling and then asserted myself and said that I had to be back at the children's home at an earlier time because we had choir practice, but it was not true. I left him drinking and swearing under his breath.

I walked back slowly, knowing it would look strange if I came back earlier than I was supposed to, so I walked for an hour or more until it seemed okay to head back. I always wondered what Francois and Petrus were doing, missing them but knowing we were all getting older and needed our own space. Francois had started "farming", as he called it, with pigeons and selling them for a good profit. He seemed happy and Petrus had a few friends with whom he sat drawing at break, so I knew he was happy, too. Well, as happy as we could be, being children's home kids and all.

Helena was sitting in the sun with her dress pulled right up so she could tan. I went to sit down next to her after I had signed in.

"How was your day with your dad?" she asked with her eyes still closed.

"Not too bad," I said. We had a moral code and family pride which made us never talk about our parents. The children would never ask each other too much, either, simply because we all lived the same lie.

She opened one eye and looked at me. "Pull your dress up so you can tan those white legs."

"No."

"Why not?"

"I hate my legs and somebody might see."

"Nobody will see, and you have beautiful legs." She closed her eyes again and rested her head against the cement wall.

"I have knob knees and hate my legs."

Now I had her attention and she grabbed my arm until I looked her straight in the face.

"Judy, my goodness, have you ever looked at your legs?"

"Yes, I have, and I hate what I see, okay?"

"Pull up your dress."

"No."

"Dammit," she murmured and pulled my dress way up.

"NO!" I shouted and jumped up and rushed inside the hostel.

Later that evening, Helena came to sit on my bed and took my hand. I was still mad at her, but left it. She looked so sincere and serious as she told me that I had to take time and look in the long mirror. She and everybody else knew I had beautiful legs and I should be proud and tuck my school dress under my belt a little for it to be shorter so I could show my legs off.

"That isn't allowed."

"Well, they won't notice if it's just a bit, and then you can show a little more of those sexy legs of yours."

I felt sad and pleaded, "Helena, I don't want sexy legs."

"Well, weird one, you have sexy legs, and if they were mine, I'd walk on my hands to show them off!"

"You are nuts!" I exclaimed and walked to the bathroom to brush my teeth. I stood in the bathroom and looked into my blue eyes. I wished I could see what Helena did. When the last girl had walked out of the bathroom, I rushed over to the long mirror. Between the cracks, I could get a good look at my legs, holding my nightdress up with my teeth and looking all around. I did not see the knobbly knees and did not know when or how they had disappeared.

Then I heard girls coming chatting into the bathroom and stopped looking straight away. I thought Helena was crazy and daring; they measured our school dresses once a week in the hall at school. When we knelt down, the hem had to be no more than four inches from the floor. I did not want to get into trouble and would not shorten my school dress under my belt.

It was Friday and, walking to school, Helena walked behind me to make sure I did not pull my dress longer where she had made me tuck it in under my belt. I felt exposed and was frightened of what might happen when they checked.

"You pull it out from under your belt when you go to have it checked!" Helena was getting fed up with me and I did not want that. "Courage, courage you need!" she would say over and over.

Nobody noticed the shorter dress or checked the length that day. Helen winked at me every time she passed me in the lines to our classes and I knew what she meant. I knew I would ask her over the weekend what to do about the bandage I managed to wrap around my chest when I went running. My breasts bounced and she would know how to prevent that without having to use the tedious bandage. My father had mentioned I needed a bra and I was horrified that everybody could see that and I wished I were a boy.

Lying on our beds on Saturday, I asked her about my problem. She sat up straight in an instant.

"What do you mean, you bandage them?"

"Just what I'm saying—I wrap them tight with a bandage and then they don't move when I run, but sometimes it slips and once I felt it slipping as I ran." I frowned and picked at the clumps of wool on the blanket. "I hate having breasts."

"You have breasts, and up with you, you're trying one of my bras on." She did not hesitate and passed her bra to me.

There were only a few children in the room with no interest in us, so I started putting the bra on.

"Gee wiz!" Helene exclaimed.

"What?" Now she had me nervous.

"My bra is nearly too small for you, Judy—you need a bra."

"I hate it," I whispered. I started feeling the salty tears in my mouth and wished myself dead.

"Judy, it's okay to have breasts, and when you run at least they'll stay in place." She knew I was anxious about this and tried to make me laugh by tickling me and chasing me around the beds.

Matron called from her flatlet that we'd better be quiet—if one of her girls woke up, all hell would be let loose.

We lay back on our beds and Helena spoke to me in a whisper. We did not want hell to be let loose. She said she would ask her mother to send me a bra; the ones they gave out at the children's home were used and that was not a good thing, she declared.

I lay with my chin in my hands, looking at her. "You know so much, yet you're a year younger than me."

"I had a mother a little longer than you."

"I suppose you're right. From the moment I came in here, my education in life stopped. I hate Saturdays in this place.

What did you do on Saturdays when you weren't here?" I asked Helena.

"Oh, lots of things—I have some great friends and we knew how to party."

"You were allowed to party?"

"I wasn't allowed anything, but I did what I wanted to do."

I could see she wasn't going to share any more and I left it. Her mother would send me a bra and I would be okay.

The next day, Matron came to me with a bra. "Here, put it on," she said, holding it out to me. It was not a new one, but it looked okay. I looked over at Helena for betraying me and stomped off to the bathroom.

"Judy, I swear I did not tell a soul!" She was talking to me through the toilet door.

"Well, how do you suppose she knew?"

"Een van die snippies het haar seker gese!" ("One of the tattle-tales must have told her!")

"Helena, I needed the one from your mother!"

"I know. I'll give her a call today."

I came out of the toilet and she gave me a hug; she said she would never do anything to harm me and I had to promise her that I believed her.

"Ek glo jou, want jy is al wat ek het." ("I believe you because you're all I have.")

"I know, I know, don't worry."

Matron entered the bathroom and asked me how it fit. I said "fine, thank you," and she told me to wash it before I wore it.

That night, I saw the moon shining on my bra, which was hanging on the back of the chair to dry. It hung sadly, wilted. I did not want to wear it and I hated my body and the changes. The dresses Mrs. A had given me long, long ago were now draping off so many other girls. I would look at the clothes and think how they had once belonged to me. They had just taken them away. The matron had scolded as I hung on to them and saw the waistline of the dress growing up to under my ribs; it was time to say goodbye to them, but they were what separated me from all these other kids. They did not have what I had had. I had felt superior in my dresses. Sadly and enviously, I would look at my dresses walking around on those kids and feel anger creep into my throat.

I lay in my bed and felt so sorry for myself, thinking of menstruation, my breasts developing, my legs that were "sexy" and my entire body changing, turning my world upside down.

It had been easier without all these things. I didn't want anybody to like my body; not even *I* liked my body—in fact, I hated it. I looked at my long, white arms in the moonlight and cried. I did not want to change into a woman; I did not want to be a woman. If I had not needed to pee, I would have wanted to sew my privates closed. I would have cut my breasts off and just do sport and run. I would have run over green mountains and over hills, just pausing long enough at a spring of water to drink, and then I would have run again, run and danced through the meadows and into a world where there were birds and animals and sunshine on my face.

But when I opened my eyes, I was still inside my jail, and the burglar bars were still there, not keeping anybody out, just keeping us in. The other fifteen beds had sleeping girls in them and my bra still smirked at me from the chair.

The train was now entering Johannesburg. This was a big city with skyscrapers and many hooligans. Francois said he would take me to Hillbrow one New Year's Eve so I could see what life was all about. I couldn't wait to spend time with Francois. I missed him. I also missed Petrus, but

Francois was so wise and I could learn so much from him. He could also protect me when he took me to discos. I was planning to live my life to the full. I wanted to see and explore, to learn and become worldly wise. If I got the job with South African Airways, I would drive to the airport every day and see people arriving from or leaving for far-away countries, the countries I wanted to visit one day. I wanted to fly to Germany, where Keith was. He had gone to study there and he told me in his letters all about the wonderful adventures he had over there.

I had met Keith in Pretoria on school vacation the previous year. I stayed with my mother while she was the matron of a boarding house where Keith rented a room. He had long hair, dark waves hanging over his shoulders. He was skinny and tall and looked like he could have been a member of a rock group. He spoke English, gently and softly; I overheard him talking to his friend. I stared at him, but when he looked back at me, it was with gentle humour in his eyes and not the lust I was used to seeing in men looking at me. I was obsessed with getting to know him and lay in the sun in the afternoons, planning how I would get to talk to him, dreaming of this rebellious-looking, tall English guy.

I did meet Keith. He was in total contrast to the rock-star type, or anyone else I had ever met. He had a gentle spirit. I had emotional highs and lows; he was even. I shouted and cried a lot; Keith never cried or fussed or raised his voice. He told me I was cute and beautiful and he laughed at my jokes. He encouraged me to study hard and dream big and then left for his own four years of study in Germany. Just before he left the country, he drove his little Mini Cooper from Pretoria to visit me in the children's home in Bloemfontein. He was given a permission slip to take me out for the day. I walked tall and proud with my hand in his the entire day and felt my heart wanting to burst with love and pride.

There was a lot of commotion in the train's passage with passengers getting their luggage together to get off in

Johannesburg. I looked out of the window and saw the thousands of train lines criss-crossing, shining in the sunlight, and the big arch of the station building approaching. We would have an hour's wait here; I would get something to eat and drink. I looked in my purse. I felt so rich with Rand piled up against each other in their own little compartment. I knew I would need new shoes for my interview. That would take all the money. My father had pushed it into my hand as I walked away from him and his little room and the smell of smoke and brown liquid booze. I felt so sorry for him. Alone in his room, I supposed now sitting the hollow deeper into his mattress and drinking more and more.

I shook my head and looked deeper among all the people shouting joy at their reunions. People hugging each other, I looked at children jumping up and down with excitement. Train conductors were rushing around, blowing whistles, and baggage carriers rolling their trolleys, eager to help. I slipped back into my green couch and felt chills run up and down my spine. I was so scared I would mess up my future. I was scared I might make mistakes and end up like my parents. I wanted to be something or somebody.

From somewhere I heard music: "In the jungle, the mighty jungle, the lion sleeps tonight..." It was so strange to hear this song coming from the platform of the train station in Johannesburg, so far from any jungle. The song reminded me of the Kruger National Park, a life long ago for me. Sometimes it felt like another person and not me at all who listened to the roar of lions at night when I could not sleep. This song was about an African parent telling the baby to hush and sleep because all was safe as the lion slept tonight. Why do so many people fear lions more than people? There is so much more to fear from people. Animals are docile until you try to penetrate their world. I also tried to be docile, but people, my parents and the authorities put in charge of me for so many years, penetrated my world and caused this anger inside me to boil and make me shake inside. I hated, I was angry.

The familiar shiver ran down my spine and I sat back again.

CHAPTER TWENTY-FOUR

Taking Another Path—A Wrong One

I decided to put everything into my ballet. I would ride off to town on my green bicycle on Wednesdays. I was now allowed to keep my bicycle locked up in a storeroom off the building and received permission to ride it to ballet. Mrs. Borstlap, the ballet teacher, thought I should come to ballet two or three times a week, but knew that the sponsor would not pay for one or two extra classes per week. So, I practised and Helena would sit on the floor, reading a book, and just look up now and again when I shouted in frustration.

"Don't be so hard on yourself!" she would say without looking away from her book she was reading.

"I have to." I struggled to get a step right. I would fall down a few times and the toe shoes would cut into the tops of my toes. I knew the blisters were bleeding, but I had to do it. This was what they said made the difference between a mediocre ballet scholar and a dancer who would go all the way. Ballet could become my ticket out of prison and take me into a new world with possibilities and a fantastic future. I had to go all the way. The inspiration boiling in my chest would be stimulated when I thought of my parents and all their drinking and not helping me get further with my life.

"Helena, look, I can do it!" I exclaimed with excitement and she slowly looked up at me with a question in her brows. I danced and she looked and clapped her hands in happy excitement as I succeeded at the difficult changes while staying in the air and then landing effortlessly on the floor and continuing the choreography without any kind of interruption, making it look easy.

"You've got it!" she said and smiled sincerely.

My ballet classes took me into town earlier and earlier. I would go to my father's place and pick up the food he left out for me, with a notebook in which we left him messages when he was not there. I read the inscriptions from Francois. He sneaked out a lot and came to pick up the dove feed my father bought for him and stacked in the corner of the room. Then he would thank my dad for the money and crackers and the chocolate milk. He would end his letter by saying "I love you".

I would also take my allocation—a little slip of paper with my name on it. A sandwich in wax wrap, a little stale but good, and a chocolate milk, too. I would draw a funny face on my note to my father and tell him "thank you" for my eats and treats and money.

One rainy day, I took the bus to ballet and not my bicycle. I got off across the street from where the ballet class was and waited for the rain to subside. I stood next to a little café. On the canopy over the door was written "The Pennywhistle Café". I could see the people eating scones piled high with cream and jam. Little silver pots of steaming tea were delivered to the tables. A girl and her mother sat near the window where I stood, and I saw them laughing as the waiter placed a plate with a golden waffle on it in front of them. Slowly, first the daughter and then her mother poured syrup meticulously over every little square hollow, and then the creamy white fluff was placed on top of all this and they smiled as the cream turned gently into liquid. I kept staring as they cut a piece and placed it in their mouths. They looked up and saw me at the window, smiled and waved at me.

I darted out from under the canopy and ran through the rain to the ballet class entrance, feeling my eyes wet with tears as I approached the door.

"Compose yourself," I said to myself a few times in my head. Luckily nobody saw the tears because my face was damp with raindrops.

The image of the mother and daughter with their golden waffles stayed in my mind for days. It tore at my heart, and at the same time, my saliva would accumulate in my mouth when I thought of the taste of those sweet treats. I could only imagine.

The following Wednesday, I arrived early on my bicycle at the Pennywhistle Café. I walked uncertainly through the door, setting off the little bells hanging on the handle. I found the little table at the window where the mother and daughter had eaten their waffles. I looked at the little yellow menu and saw that I had enough money in my pocket. I ordered the waffle with cream and started biting my nails in anticipation. Nobody paid me any attention, but I felt like I was doing the biggest thing in my entire life. I was in a café by myself and ordering something to eat all by myself. This was nearly normal; this made me feel nearly normal. I looked around at the other tables. The man with the newspaper did not even look up.

Then, my heaven arrived. I stared at the golden waffle. I said "thank you" and touched it with my finger. Warm. I poured, as meticulously as the mother and daughter had, the syrup into the golden square ponds and then the cream, and then a little more. The first bite in my mouth made my eyes water. I felt happy and amazed at the same time. I could not believe my taste buds as the golden dream disappeared fast in my mouth.

The last piece I ate slowly, then I looked at my empty plate. I scraped the last bit of syrupy cream onto my fork and then I saw the woman behind the counter looking at me so I pushed my plate hastily away. None of the raw pain and joy should show outwardly. This was my secret; they did not know where I came from. I was a normal person eating a waffle in a café.

I paid with my crumpled Rand notes and walked out fast, pushing my bicycle to the ballet class.

This venture became my obsession, and the staff at the Pennywhistle came to know exactly what I would order every time. My entire week would be absorbed with a way to get enough money together to eat my weekly waffle. My father would ask me what I did with the money he gave me occasionally, but I didn't tell him I just wanted the money.

Sometimes my father would leave me a few coins next to a note from him in our little communication notebook. I would thank him and not take the snack he also laid out.

Instead I would eat my waffle, meticulously, from side to side, and then place my knife and fork neatly next to each other when I was finished. Then it was ballet.

One Wednesday, I walked past the Pennywhistle. My father had been lying drunk in his room when I went there and there was no money or snack.

I could not buy a waffle that day. I walked with my eyes glued to the pavement, looking for lost coins, especially along the pavement where the parking meters were. I was early and walked into the ballet class to watch the lesson before mine. One of the older girls sent me to her school blazer pocket to find her some bobby pins for her hair. I walked to the changing room and found her blazer, slipped my hand in the pocket and felt loose change in my hand. I pulled it out and then threw it back and handed her the bobby pins.

I started biting my nails because I knew I could get the money out of the many pockets in the changing room.

I did.

I had money for a waffle now and again. My father was still not giving me any, and I was obsessed with going to the Pennywhistle.

One day I stuck my hand into some girl's pocket and pulled a one-Rand note out and a senior girl stood in the door and asked me what I was doing in her blazer pocket. Startled, I said I thought it was somebody else's and I was looking for bobby pins.

The next week, the Reverend called me to his office. I knew. He made me stand in front of him and asked if I had stolen money at the ballet school. I said I had not. He said I had been found out. I denied it. He became angry and called me a pathetic example and ambassador for the children's home. At that, he took out a long cane. He made me stand bent forward, holding onto his desk, and he whipped me ten strokes. I cried and was humiliated, but thought this was my punishment and I should take it. I promised myself, with every stroke as it hit into my body with such excruciating pain, that I would never, never take anything from anybody as long as I lived. He stood looking directly into my eyes and hissed that it was the last of my ballet classes, because I was a thief, a disgusting thief!

I was empty. I was finished. I had thought the hiding was my punishment, not taking away my ballet. I cried all the time and made up illnesses, trying to stay in my bed. I stopped eating. I was so embarrassed and did not find a cross of Jesus anywhere and if I did, I tried not to see it. I told everybody that the sponsor could not pay for my ballet anymore. But the truth and the pain stung my heart forever. I was a thief. Self-hatred stepped into my life. I could not stand to look at myself. I avoided my reflection in the mirror. A cloud covered my eyes and my life and I became just another girl in the home.

Sadness overcame my entire being, with intervals of bitter, bitter anger. I felt the struggle of life boiling in my head and I wished I could end it all.

Francois, Petrus and I left the children's home gates that morning, with my father driving his newly attained Anglia. We left happy and in expectation of a day away from hell. My father was only slightly drunk and even allowed Francois to drive the car for a while, to my brother's utmost pleasure. I looked at his reflection in the rear-view mirror; he had this wide grin and his eyes were the blue of the sky. Then my father had a bit more to drink and, as he took some sharp turns, he sang "On a Wing and a Prayer" from his World War days, when he had been in the Air Force in St. Helena. He drove happily and we saw more of Bloemfontein than we ever had. We went up to Naval Hill and enjoyed the view of the city.

Later, when my father was fiercely drunk and Francois decided to pour his liquor down the drain, everything went wrong. Francois' chin turned red-purple after my father hit him and he went running out of the door with Petrus and me after him. We walked to the children's home in the dark and I tried to tell Francois that he had been so brave to pour that disgusting stuff down the drain. His chin did not look good; we stopped at a garden tap so he could pour a little water over it. I walked alone after the boys had disappeared into their hostel.

I was on the outside, looking into the boys' hostel. In one room, I could see two boys sitting on their beds, playing some card game. Through another window, I saw a boy hanging his washed school socks over his chair to dry. A small boy was standing, crying his heart out, and nobody paid him any attention. I walked on the roadside pavement towards my hostel, tears running down my cheeks, and felt like I could just keep on walking forever and never return. I did not want to go behind those bars anymore. I felt defeated and tired. I had been locked up so long. I lifted my chin a little and thought that although I was locked up, I should never lose my soul.

*   *   *

Bloody dammit! I was sitting waiting for the train to leave Johannesburg station so I could get started with my life.

I had succeeded in messing up a part of my life all by myself. Not only had the people in my life hurt and damaged me, but I had carried on where they left off. I had caused myself to stoop down to them, join them: *let's see who can kill her spirit, if not her.*

I could have had a great career through my biggest dream, being a ballet dancer. A prima ballerina. That was the hope in the eyes of all the girls who had a passion, who weren't doing ballet just because their mommies wanted them to, in whose eyes you could see the passion blazing raw. In control of the ballet steps, with determination, never satisfied until it was perfect. Always striving for perfection from the top of their head through the ends of their fingers and in total control throughout the body, ending in the pointed toe.

From the time following the moment I stopped doing ballet, a part of my life stopped, too. I did laugh again, but without the extra spark; I did enjoy, but without the intensity; I did succeed, but never in my ballet. I removed that from my life by myself and would never be able to forgive myself. The shame and humiliation clung to my being. I felt I could never ever eat a waffle again in my life because it always reminded me of what I had done.

Mrs. Alexander had a way of calling my name, playfully rhyming and changing it until it became Judas. Judy, Judas, Judah, Judas Iscariot. I was that: I was the betrayer; I had betrayed myself. I know Judas hung himself; the Bible says so, but I was even too weak to do that.

I had to get off this train and begin a new life.

A few of the last people on the platform started moving away and the bustle calmed down. The train started out of the station with a little bump, moving a few metres backwards, and then another little bump and then the moving forward began. I had to move forward, too.

I could never sabotage myself again. I had to stop biting my nails and I should get a map of the world to study countries and some general knowledge on political issues, because at this interview we might be asked questions. I had to be prepared and walk up straight and lift my chin a little higher and look sincerely back at the panel interviewers.

I was eighteen years old and I wanted to work as a ground hostess for three years, and then I would be old enough to apply to become an air hostess. That was my ultimate dream. I would see the world and fly away as far as possible from all the hurt, pain and disgust of my past. I would walk with my hostess uniform, all proud, in my little hat and white gloves and the beautiful scarf draped around my neck, and passers-by would admire me and I would be seen as one of the special elite of South African Airways, one of those select few. People would smile when they saw me walk by, because I would represent the holiday far, far away of which they were dreaming. I smiled and could envision myself in this new world.

I ended my school with the Matriculation High school dance. I proudly made my own dress and had a guy at my side, one with lust in his eyes, which I ignored. Francois was out of school, Petrus left to live with my mother, Helena left to live with her mother, and eventually I ended my time in the home all by myself.

I was living for letters from Keith telling me about Europe. The letters were opened, as always, by the children's home office. They read our letters first and then placed a little sticky tape over the opening; it was censored and then passed on to us.

I pasted a calendar with the last four months above my bed and I deleted each day with a big black X until the last day in the children's home, when I greeted the girls and the matron with a salute and a very big smile. I'd seen so many people leave here crying, as if they were leaving behind some dear loved one. I had no tears, no sadness. I walked towards the home's transport, which waited to take me to the train station. I held my suitcase tightly in my hand and I never looked back at the burglar bars.

CHAPTER TWENTY-FIVE

My Life Thirty-Two Years Later

I see the green of the leaves on the trees bobbing by. I have tears in my eyes as I jog along the path. My eyelashes glisten in the sun. I cannot run and cry, so I stop and listen to my breathing: a healthy heart, a healthy, strong body. God has been good to my body. I am as strong as I was at eighteen. I've put on a bit of weight. I laugh and make the easy excuse that it's because of the good life in the United States of America, the country of abundance!

Ironically, I am running along the Silver Comet trail in Atlanta. It was a railroad some time ago.

I sit on a rock and wave at some cyclists flying by. How did I get here? How can I feel so normal? The only tears are from happiness. Keith and I have been married twenty-nine years today. Our beautiful children are twenty-seven and twenty-three years old.

When I run I feel so strong, but for years I ran away and not towards. I remember what happened.

CHAPTER TWENTY-SIX

My Pillow Children

I start running again. I have always hoped that one day I would run towards and not away from. The more I think, the faster I run.

My past is behind me and now I have a life. I can live, breathe and enjoy.

Other joggers run past me, chatting. They smile and wave. I am just one of the joggers on the Silver Comet. I am nearly normal. I am just another normal person.

I pretended to be normal for as long as my own children were in the house. I never knew how to raise children, but I knew if I did everything opposite to what had been done to me, I would be fine.

So, when I became angry, I changed my attitude. When something was spilled, I did not scream—it was an accident. And so on.

Then, love.

Oh, I loved.

I love my children.

Now I want to cry again, but you cannot run and cry; I know that now.

I love my children in ways I cannot explain. I held them much tighter. I kissed them for no reason at all and all over, and all the time.

I placed their whole little baby foot into my mouth, and as they cried out in laughter, I cried with joy.

I played with them, looking at their toys with the same joy and amusement as they would.

I touched them at every moment, when just walking past them.

I smelt them.

I traced my finger over their beautifully perfect little profiles.

I bathed them in thousands of baby-smelling bubbles and I lifted their clean, wet bodies into soft folds of fluffy towels.

I held them, smelling and kissing into their necks.

When they left for school in the morning, I stood in their rooms or just sat on their beds missing them. I packed their school lunch in abundance with a little note written on their napkin.

I was the first parent waiting at the school gate for them. I was never late; I would always be there when the end-of-day school bell rang out. My heart skipped a beat as I recognised them among the other little heads.

I cooked for them like little black Rosa cooked. I told them animal stories like Mr. Cilliers could. I taught them respect for Africa and love for all creatures, as Piet in the Kruger National Park had told me. I managed to remember my witch doctor's stories and helped my children understand that people have different beliefs and we should respect them.

I helped them show empathy to people of all races and extra to those who have less than we do.

I had bowls of fruit overflowing onto the kitchen table, available for any little hunger pang, and they could choose a favourite candy or packet of crisps in the corner café where I bought our bread.

They loved our black Constance's motherly arms as much I did. We all went dead quiet as she sang her Jesus songs while helping us with our chores, or as she stood ironing.

Constance smelled of eucalyptus and, in her embrace, we would inhale her peaceful love.

I made my children find the fairies in our garden and I watched, holding my breath with them, as they stepped high and careful so as not to disturb the sleeping pixies.

My angel children coloured outside the lines as we did art on rainy days when we could not lie outside and stare into blue-sky days, forming pictures out of the fluffy white clouds. My two pillow-corner children became real-life children. My life. My love.

CHAPTER TWENTY-SEVEN
My Mother

She stood on the platform as the train pulled into Pretoria Station. I saw her standing neatly dressed, blowing the cigarette smoke out, waving when she saw me. She worked in the kitchen of the Magnolia Clinic and we were going to share a two-bedroom apartment on the premises. My mother warned me that I had to enrol Petrus in high school at the end of the month; she could not take any leave from work.

It dawned on me that I would have to do a lot of things. I might not be able to concentrate solely on my new life. She spoke hurriedly and we walked fast towards the bus stop. She was late for her shift because my train had been delayed.

The transition was not at all as I had expected. My moments of real freedom were when I sat in the library and studied the many maps of the world. In the quiet stuffiness of the library, I could escape and touch books for as long as I liked.

My mother and I had so many fights. She mentioned that I was driving her back into the arms of liquor and I cringed, wishing I could be somewhere else.

I had two weeks after I arrived in Pretoria to prepare myself for the interview.

It was with a racing heart that I purchased my bus ticket for the South African Airways terminal. I sat on the bus very carefully so as not to crease my skirt. My mother had ironed it twice for me. I had washed and dried my hair into a bun. Little bits of hair would not reach the bun and curled around my face. I looked at my nails; I had tried not to put them near my mouth, and in the fighting fits my mother and I had had over the last weeks, I would sit on my hands and bite the inside of my mouth.

I tied an autumn-coloured scarf around my neck, just like I would when I wore the uniform; hopefully the panel would see the resemblance and approve. I was so nervous. I clung to my brown envelope with all my references. One sheet was my high school certificate. One was a letter from Reverend van Rooyen, explaining that I had been a pleasure at the children's home and that I had a good background with excellent ethics and would be an asset to anybody who wanted to employ me.

I had nearly left this letter behind because it might jeopardise my chances. They would wonder about a child raised in a children's home.

A handful of us were asked to stay behind after our initial interview and I realised I might have a chance. We were called in again one by one. They approved of me.

The sky turned blue. The sun shone on my face and I smiled with such pride as I purchased my return ticket for the bus to Pretoria. I belonged to this elite airline.

My mother was sincerely happy for me, but during our first argument, she said I thought I was something special and better than her because I now worked for an airline.

I looked at her as the foam formed at the corners of her mouth. She shouted, her brown eyes blazing, that I reminded her of my disgusting father. I screamed back and it felt good. She told me how terrible my personality was and that I looked down on her. She walked straight up into my face and spat as she screamed. I did what I could never do before: I walked out of the door and down the street to nowhere for a long time.

After I started working at South African Airways, my mother would iron my skirts in the evenings after her shift in the hospital until it was perfect, with not one crease. She looked proud of me when I was dressed in my uniform.

I would come home after work, too tired to eat the food she left me, and we would fight. I heard her telling Petrus that I was trying to be better than her, that her food was not good enough for me.

She ironed my white blouses until they stood in perfection and brightness.

My first salary was a treasure. I cashed the cheque and opened a bank account. I stood outside the bank and felt as high as the clouds. I felt rich; I was becoming normal. I walked past the shop windows and looked at all the things I was able to buy. I looked at all the clothes and imagined buying them. I could if I wanted to. I smiled.

When I walked into the apartment, I smelt it. Alcohol. I cringed and looked at my mother, slumped in a chair at the little kitchenette.

"Ag nee!" ("oh no!") Was all I could say as I put my handbag on the chair.

"Don't, Judy—just don't!" she whispered, frightening me. She smiled at me with saliva dripping from her lips. "Did you get your first salary cheque?" she enquired.

I nodded. I did not have a purse, so the lady at the bank had given me a little plastic bag with the bank logo on it.

"How much did you get?" she asked.

"Quite a lot," I said proudly, and showed her the little plastic bag.

"You'll have to pay for your food from next month, Judy. The kitchen will see when I take an extra plate off to the apartment."

"I want to give you some money now already, Mammie. I want you to buy yourself a new frock."

She frowned at me and said she did not need a new frock. To where would she wear it and for whom did she need to look nice? All she did was work and work. She had no life. Then she cried, grabbed her bottle and glass and stormed off into her room, slamming the door.

We were a very angry family. I screamed, my mother screamed, Petrus kicked stuff and screamed, too.

But I could not help myself: I screamed at her through the closed door and told her to drink and drink until she fell over and then she could get up and drink again, for all I cared.

I had nowhere to go, but I needed to get out. It was dark outside but I changed quickly and walked out of the door. I could get fish and chips at the corner café, but where would I eat it? I couldn't go to the Library; it was closed. I didn't know anybody.

I walked into the twenty-four-hour pharmacy and looked at lipsticks. I bought my very first purchase with my own earned money. I walked back into the apartment and climbed into my bed and cried. This could not be what I had left the children's home for.

She drank on and off for the next few weeks, and every time I touched the door handle of the apartment, it was with my heart beating heavy in my chest. When she was sober and the place was clean and my Airways outfit washed and ironed to perfection, I was so relieved that I chatted too much, smiled a lot and kept Petrus and myself busy with card games so she could relax, with the hope that things would stay just like this.

I would walk into the apartment and smell the disgusting alcohol entering my nostrils, causing tears to form in my eyes, the disappointment of my hopeful expectation swallowed with the booze.

I looked at the pathetic person slumped, careless, in the chair or on her bed. I would scrub myself in the bath and cry and bite my nails until they bled. Petrus would go about his things, needing me to get home so I could see what had happened. It looked like fear, anger and disappointment in his brown eyes as he busied himself with his things. I was too sorry for myself to find pity for him in my heart as well. So I would ask him if he had food and leave him to do what he did.

I found alternative accommodation in a hostel for Christian ladies in Sunnyside and signed my name on the application form.

I left my mother and Petrus with an explanation that I needed my own space. My mother stood sober in front of me and told me I would still bump my head very hard for refusing a giving hand. She told me how she slaved over my ironing and how she gave me her plate of food every day. I cried and begged her not to say all these mean things to me.

Her last words, as I walked away with my own apartment key burning in my hand, were, "Ek sal jou nooit vergewe wat jy vandag aan my doen nie en die nagevolge is jou skuld" ("I will never forgive you for what you're doing to me today, and the consequences will be your fault"). I told her I would not be far away and shifted my suitcase from one hand to the other. I gave my mother some money and knew I would have to walk to my new accommodation.

I unlocked my door and walked over to the window, past a single bed, nightstand and desk with chair. Bare but clean. Mine, all mine. At last I was alone. I packed my clothes in the wardrobe and realised I would have to buy an iron. I lay on my bed and listened to my own breathing. I said out loud, "Hello, Judy" and again "Hello, hello, hello, dis ek, dis Judy" ("it's me, it's Judy").

I smiled at my silliness and jumped up off the bed and took another look at my little bathroom. I smiled, put the lights off, ran on my tiptoes to my bed and jumped in. I smiled and thought of the list of things I would have to buy. Toilet paper; soap, for clothes and body. I jumped out of the bed again and found a piece of paper and pen and made a list.

1) Toilet paper (two rolls until the end of the month)

2) Toilet soap (nice smelly one—rose fragrance, preferably)

3) Soap powder for clothes

4) Iron

5) Alarm clock

6) Ironing board—next month. I will iron on my bed for now

7) Toothpaste (nice-tasting one)

8) Pantyhose for work (three pairs)

9) Clear nail varnish (to stop ladders in pantyhose and for nails)

10) Milk powder and coffee

11) Kettle

12) Instant soup packets (tomato soup)

13) Vim to clean my bathroom with

14) Anything I can cook on the two-plate stove (will have to look)

I smiled as I looked at my window. There were no burglar bars. I found a star in the sky.

The train had stopped. I had arrived and I was free; I could decide my path of life.

I was now responsible for myself and my walk into the future. I touched my pillow. This building was new and so were the bare essentials with which it was furnished. New mattress, one pillow, one set of new sheets and a pale blue blanket, soft. I was the first person to sleep in this little room. It was brand new and I could still smell the fresh paint. I rubbed my hands over the soft blanket.

I pushed my head deeper into the clean, soft pillow and sighed.

I smiled a little more and fell asleep.

CHAPTER TWENTY-EIGHT

My Father's Denial

I was working at the desk in the South African Airways building, proudly, issuing tickets to the passengers for their flights to far-away countries. I had studied all the places around the world—not only the capital cities and the main attractions, but small details I could tell my passengers as they sat eagerly on the other side of my desk, waiting for me to write out their entire itinerary. I was as excited as they were. I would look at them and tell them not to forget to buy some beautiful embroidered tablecloths at the market in Budapest. They should make sure to buy these beautiful pieces from the gypsies and not forget to bargain for a good price. They would smile as they accepted their envelope with all their travel documents and my heart would go along with them on their tour.

I was somebody behind this desk and felt so good that I had succeeded in getting a position in Pretoria's city office. I went on every course offered by the airline and could now work in any area. I had worked for the airline for one year and enjoyed every day. I was planning my first vacation to Durban in December. The airline gave us one free air ticket and a good discount at the Malibu hotel once a year. It would be my first time on a plane and I was so excited.

On a warm November afternoon, a thunderstorm was brewing outside. I had a free moment and sat looking outside. The world was turning a deep purple and I knew it was going to rain soon.

Two policemen arrived at my desk and asked if I was Judy van der Walt. I nodded.

"Could you follow us outside?" one enquired.

My heart skipped a beat. Outside, they told me in a whisper that I needed to walk with them around the corner to the Poyntens building. My father was on the eleventh floor, wanting to jump.

I started shaking and felt my throat close up.

"Why?" was all I could whisper; the men didn't even hear me.

We arrived at the south side of the building, just in time to see my father being placed in the back of a police van. I asked if I could speak to him. He seemed drunk and bewildered.

"Hoekom het pappie dit nou wou doen?" ("Why did you want to do that?")

"Ek het niks om voor te lewe nie" ("I have nothing to live for"). He told me that he had come all the way to live in Pretoria and did not even see his own kids. I felt guilty. I did not visit him; he was right, he had called me when he moved to Pretoria six months ago, but I was too scared to face him: too many memories, and the bigger fear of seeing him drunk.

The policeman told us to finish up, as he had to take my father for evaluation at the hospital. When the policeman moved away, my father whispered that he was sorry for what he had done to me as a child. My head shot up. I looked into his watery blue eyes. I knew exactly what he was talking about.

"It was terrible!" I croaked through my pressed-together lips. My heart was pounding in my temples; I felt like fainting and grabbed the side of the van.

"I know and I'm sorry," he said, looking down at his hands.

"I will never get over it," I whispered.

"You must remember one thing." He was now speaking in a low, threatening voice. "I never, ever penetrated you, NEVER!"

"And I should be grateful for that?" I spat the words out and felt the tears of anger in my eyes, which I wiped hastily away with the back of my hand.

The policeman came over, hearing us talking loudly, and said they were going and I should move away from the van so he could lock it up.

My father drove off in the back of the van, holding onto the bars as they went around the corner. I just stood there. I could not move. A crowd had formed around the spectacle and I stood in blasphemy in my beautiful South African Airways uniform.

Dirty and found out. I was not what my uniform helped me pretend I was.

I was just rubbish, pathetic, like my family.

CHAPTER TWENTY-NINE

Eliminating the Pain One By One

My mother became sober, but I stayed scared. She "slipped" when Michelle, my daughter, was born in 1980, when I think my little girl reminded her of how badly she wanted to be normal, sober.

There would be three generations of us, sitting outside, drinking tea in my beautiful garden. Keith bought us a brand new house on the outskirts of Pretoria and Michelle had a perfect pink and brown baby room. I played house and put lipstick on when Keith arrived home from work. He would play with Michelle and I would dish our supper up and we would sit at the dining room table with Michelle in her high chair. My heart overflowed.

My mother played in the sandpit with Michelle and they both laughed and I saw the tears in my mother's eyes. This little girl had saved her life.

Then Michael was born and she loved being a grandmother of two. I could see it in her eyes when she looked at them.

My two normal children could easily throw their arms around necks to hand out kisses because they were so filled with love.

We moved into our next house with a thatched roof, swimming pool and beautiful view of Pretoria East.

I stayed concerned and worried about my mother. I cleaned her little apartment. I bought her frocks. I visited, as much as I could; we were all she had.

I called her to hear if her voice was sober or not. I called her every second day. I was disappointed a few times and I cried.

I always hoped she would become happy within herself, but it was hard. She was worried about Francois and Petrus. Francois drank too much. Petrus had his own demons at that stage.

My mother never asked me for money, but I knew she needed it, so I gave as much as I could; I went without so she could have, always wondering how much of my money went to feed her addiction.

I did love my mother. In my way, I did. I was so sorry for her most of the time. I wanted her to hug and hold me, but I also made my back stiff when she did try. I kissed her only in order to smell if she had alcohol on her breath. When she did not, I felt like I could live in peace, breathe for a while. When she did, I fled and did not feel guilty as I tried to live my own life, trying not to make the same mistakes.

Her dream was to move to Cape Town, back to her roots, and when she finally did, I heard her voice was happy because she was near the sea. She stayed in a retirement village and she was eager to show her little apartment to us.

My mother died suddenly one day in 1991 of a heart attack while waiting for her blood pressure prescription at the pharmacy. It was two months before we could visit her with the children that December vacation, but I know she was happy at last. She did little chores for the older ladies where she lived.

I do not have to call my mother anymore, to listen with a beating heart if she is sober or not, but I know she saw me when I buried the letter of forgiveness at her graveside.

She would love the fact that we now live in the United States of America, because she told me once that she named me after the famous Hollywood star, Judy Garland.

CHAPTER THIRTY
My Father

The goodbye to my father as he lay dead in a pulled-out drawer, inside that plastic bag, was the end to his life, but it was not the end of my pain; maybe it was just the beginning. It was the summer of 1993.

I had had to sign for the surgery to remove a first organ in hospital. He was in intensive care in Pretoria and I was the only family member they could reach for approval. I remember looking at him: he was a yellow colour and very angry. They had to tie his hands down because he was ripping the place apart. I questioned the doctor and he told me it was the morphine making my father so wild. With all the tubes in his mouth and nose, he could not speak, but his blue eyes asked so many questions I could not answer.

The following week, they called me to sign again, for more surgery. I dropped the children at their schools and left for a long day at the hospital. I would have to stay to see if he got through this surgery as well—it sounded serious.

I sat in the waiting room, trying to force my memories away from myself being alone with my father as a child. I still had so many nightmares and fears, so much guilt and anger. How would I look at my father without thinking of what he had done to my childhood?

The nurse asked me to sign some consent form for the surgery.

"What type of surgery is this?" I asked as I looked over the official hospital consent form.

"Oh, I thought you knew—your father's cancer has spread into his testicles and they will have to be removed." The nurse scratched under her little white cap with a pen as she spoke.

"No!" I squeaked.

"Are you okay?" The nurse looked at me, misunderstanding my outburst as concern for my father.

"I have to sign on this form that his testicles may be removed?" I felt all the blood drain out of my face.

"Yes, do you have an objection?" The nurse was puzzled. "It's really important if he wants to live."

"No," I squeaked, even softer. I needed air. "Can I get some water?"

"Yes, take your time—the bathroom is down the corridor, and then you can come to the nurses' desk and I'll have you sign." She walked off.

I put my face over the basin and poured cold water into my hands. I was shaking severely. I patted some water on my face and looked at my reflection in the mirror. My freckles lay splattered over the pale of my face and I felt the tears run over my cheeks. This couldn't be happening. I looked up at the fluorescent light in the ceiling and asked if God could please help me now for a change. This was too big for me.

I walked firmly to the nurses' desk. There the nurse stood laughing with a patient who was checking out, arranging help with all the flowers she needed to be carried. I panicked and wanted to return to the bathroom. But what if I took too long and my father died because I did not sign in time for the surgery? What if I signed and this surgery killed my father?

I took the pen in my right hand. I stared at the scar still visible on my hand, the hand I had wanted to cut off in shame, so many years ago. This hand was now going to remove my father's testicles.

I sat in the little chapel in the corridor with an empty head. I started to shiver. I could envision the doctor cutting off one and then the other testicle. I looked at the cross. I spoke to the cross. *I did not do it. He did it to himself. He has ruined his body with all the drinking and smoking. He chose the lifestyle he did and the brown liquor he poured down his throat must have taken its toll.*

I was quiet then. I was sorry but not guilty.

I stood up and walked over to the cross.

I stretched my right hand out in front of me and looked at it. I touched the wooden cross at the front of the chapel and then I rubbed my hand over the smooth of it. I rubbed the wooden cross with my right hand and sighed. It was over. "Your will be done." I whispered.

My father did not die that day; he died three months later, when he drank himself into a stupor and landed back in hospital with pneumonia. I only signed at the hospital morgue that I identified him. It was him lying in the plastic bag, his face distorted. It was my father.

I burned all his pornography on a sunshine day outside my house, I watched the flames engulf every page and looked as the smoke spiralled into the sky and knew with certainty I would never forget, but I forgave him as the last of the ash blew into the wind.

Epilogue

I run.

I see the path in front my feet bobbing up and down.

I remember how hard it was for me to trust anybody.

I run and the cement path in front of my shoes is swallowed by my pushing forward, I have always pushed forward.

My iPod explodes with the voice singing in my ear, how hard it was for me to never stray too far from the sidewalk, to trust not only me, but also everyone around me.

I have learnt the hard way. I don't think my heart was ever whole to start with! A baby cutting blades into her flesh is abnormal, and I know it now.

I live with normal now, so I know how out of whack my entire childhood was.

I cry.

I cannot run further.

I stop and sit beside the path, panting and crying with my head in my arms.

I sob for the loss of a childhood.

I smile at the sky in thanksgiving.

Keith, who held me so tight, against his chest the thousands of times as the waves of anger or sadness exploded inside me. He taught me gentleness with the humour, which fill our house with loud laughter and arguments.

I think I am becoming normal.

I crawl to a tree and sit with my back against the hard bark. The grass is wet; it smells like cucumbers, clean and fresh.

I have to forgive in order to move on. This could be my last step, or crawl. I know that.

I have such a little way still to go until I will stand on that mountaintop without a trace of pain.

I fall into the kneeling position. My head touches the damp ground and I grab hold of a clump of wet grass. I rock back and forth, crying and praying. I need this pain to stop. I am so happy now. I will never forget my past, neither the people who played a role in it, but I forgave those who have done me wrong. I can live now, no regrets.

I stare into the bluest sky above me with wet eyes and know with certainty that the pain has ended.

I become calm and look down to the ground and then I see it. Amongst the leaves on the ground, I see a cross: two little twigs lying in front of my teary eyes, not the cross in the burglar bars, just gently lying there, a perfect little formation of the cross in the freedom of life.

"Jesus, oh Jesus," I breathe, and move on.